Wow! This book is a tremendous of life. My eyes have been opened to Jesus' journey through suffering as a timeless guide. This book brings a faithful forecast: a storm is brewing and headed my way. In this world, I will have trouble (John 16:33).

For me as a leader, these are brilliant insights into Jesus' journey to (and through!) suffering. The pages come alive with valuable tools as I prepare myself and others for the often painful path of life. This book contains practical truths for this life that will be rewarded for all eternity. This is a must read for Christian leaders who would prepare themselves and others for the storms of life. They are approaching; now I am prepared!

ROBERT C. MCCLELAND, PHD
EXECUTIVE DIRECTOR AND CEO
NORTH AMERICAN BAPTIST CONVENTION

While reading this book, we are navigating our own personal "perfect storm" through a crisis in our business. The insights Bob Wenz brings from the Scripture and from his own experience greatly help us focus on the greatness of God and his power, majesty, and love—and rejoice through what he is doing in our lives. This book helps us keep "kedging" as God directs our passage through this storm.

Bob Wenz's words offered us great comfort and strength when he reminded us that *Our antidote for anxiety in the midst of difficulty is rooted in our trust in the promises of Jesus. That is not an expression of mere fideism or "faith in faith." We must also believe what Jeremiah recorded as God's promise: "I know the plans I have for you, plans to prosper you and not to harm you, plans to give you hope and a future" (Jer. 29:11).*

BILL FORSYTHE
CEO, FORSYTHE TRANSPORTATION
GAINESVILLE, TX

In his provocative and informative study on coaching through times of crisis, Robert Wenz provides God's inviting portrait of how Jesus navigates his unprecedented and unparalleled life crisis. Crises come in various shapes and sizes and never seem to let up. Drawing upon his rich experience as a pastor for nearly thirty years, Bob began to see how Jesus' crash course on navigating his life crisis (in John 13–16) prepared his disciples for the inevitable crises they would face as his followers. Accordingly, *Navigating Your Perfect Storm* is not a series of sermons or a how-to self-help book, but a set of reflections, insights, and illustrations—based on the seminar notes that John took on our behalf— for those who seek to follow Jesus today. As our world increasingly crumbles into pieces, Jesus offers peace for those who deploy his anchors and heed his admonitions.

An insightful, authentic, beautiful, rare, and exciting book with a moving style! This is a real book about the real world, written with warm human understanding and witty perspective. It will, and should, help many of us navigate our life crises.

DR. WESLEY M. PINKHAM
DEAN OF DOCTORAL STUDIES
THE KING'S COLLEGE AND SEMINARY

As a child of God suffering an incurable disease, Bob Wenz artfully uses Jesus' upper room discourse to dissect and understand his own "trail of tears." His reflections assist the rest of us who struggle with the difficulties of migrating through this life.

JIM GRIFFITH
GRIFFITH COACHING
DENVER, COLORADO

Bob Wenz has graciously given us a "psalm of his life." This valuable narrative does not allow us to become anchored to political or personal crises. Bob has had enough of each. In his clear teaching from Jesus' words, he points us to spiritual maturity that celebrates each potential obstacle on our journey home.

DR. ARTHUR EVANS GAY
MCHENRY, ILLINOIS

In this superb work on Jesus' final counsel to his close followers, Dr. Wenz blends scholarly study with poignant metaphors. With transparency, the author shares his own personal journey and how Jesus' teaching is impacting his perspective on an uncertain future. The reader can expect to be drawn deeply into the unique comfort, hope, and perspective that Jesus came to provide for his followers.

DOUG BARRAM
BEND, OR

A perfect storm awaits all of us—whether it's a financial meltdown, family blowups, or a sick or dying child. How we respond shows ourselves, and others, something deeply significant about our faith. Bob Wenz's new book is helping me navigate my storm with courage, and his book is certain to help many others pass boldly through theirs.

TOM HESS
MAGAZINE EDITOR
(FORMER EDITOR, *CITIZEN* MAGAZINE)

Navigating Your Perfect Storm is true. My friend, Bob Wenz, is suffering from an incurable disease, so he knows something about dealing with the most difficult questions of life and death. Having had to face and survive my own storm of humiliation, judgment, and rejection, I know something about embracing godly ideals that seem at times to conflict with reality. Though Bob's perfect storm is being imposed upon him and mine was self-inflicted, the disappointment and questions are the same. This book is pragmatic, yet thoroughly biblical, and communicates Bob's wise insights through his clever personality. I encourage all to not just read this book but to ingest it. It is excellent, worthy of careful study and thought.

TED HAGGARD
PASTOR, ST. JAMES CHURCH
COLORADO SPRINGS, CO

NAVIGATING YOUR PERFECT STORM

NAVIGATING YOUR
PERFECT STORM

DR. BOB WENZ

Biblica Publishing
We welcome your questions and comments.

USA   1820 Jet Stream Drive, Colorado Springs, CO 80921
India   Logos Bhavan, Medchal Road, Jeedimetla Village, Secunderabad
         500 055, A.P.

Navigating Your Perfect Storm
ISBN-13: 978-1-60657-099-9

12 11 10 / 6 5 4 3 2 1

Published in 2010 by Biblica Publishing

A catalog record for this book is available through the Library of Congress.

Printed in the United States of America

For Bill and Adel, no strangers to adversity, whose kindness and generosity made it possible for me to write.

CONTENTS

FOREWORD

I personally enjoy reading a book that stimulates me to follow Jesus more passionately and one that deepens my understanding of my life in Christ. *Navigating Your Perfect Storm* accomplishes both of these objectives by making me want to be a fervent follower of Jesus and opening up new dimensions of insight that stir my soul.

Bob Wenz is a superb teacher, but what he brings most to this book is years of experience as a pastor tempered in the fire of suffering. He has seen suffering, and now he lives his own personal experience in the crucible of pain. The combination of gifting, experience, and pain forms this book into a well-rounded primer on following Jesus. This book is no simple "how to" formula but rather a well of wisdom that points to key signposts on the journey of the life in Christ.

I first met Bob when we were both members of South Park Church in Park Ridge, Illinois. At the time we were both young and energetic. We were part of a generation that believed we could change the world in our generation. Now almost forty years later we are more sober in our optimism, but nevertheless confident that God is indeed at work in our world doing some amazing things.

Our optimism is now tempered with the knowledge that this world is full of complexities and circumstances that cause painful suffering and trials in the world. Navigating these difficulties is so important for us as disciples of Jesus. Bob's discussions on identity, authority, the Word and truth, prayer, etc., take us into life issues in a way that helps us see how Jesus has instructed us to deal with suffering and difficulties. His handling of key passages of the upper room discourse is masterful. He is able to take Jesus' instruction and open our eyes to profound understanding of these texts.

I absolutely love how he deals with Jesus' strong sense of identity. He then applies Jesus' experiences to our own lives and helps us understand how our own sense of identity in Christ grounds us to live life. Unless our identity is strongly anchored in who we are in Christ, we will struggle mightily.

This book requires careful meditation as it is read. Each illustration amplifies exposition that is well thought through. Each chapter builds on the previous chapter, and the book as a whole is held together by the theme of dealing with the trials and complexities of life. While it is not written in language that is difficult to grasp, the content is thoughtful and deep. No one will be disappointed if they carefully and prayerfully read this book.

My prayer is that everyone who reads this book will be as deeply blessed and challenged as I have been. I praise God for Bob's life, his gift for teaching and writing, his wisdom, and above all his transparency. May his life lessons be passed on to many of us as we read this book.

Alan Andrews
Former U.S Director of the Navigators

INTRODUCTION
ARRESTED

We never anticipate what seemingly small things can significantly change our lives. In the summer of 1998, I received a call from a director in the National Office of the Christian and Missionary Alliance, my denomination. Dr. Paul Bubna, the president of the denomination, had died suddenly of a heart attack that spring. We were all stunned and saddened at the loss of an outstanding man and leader. Little did I know what Paul's passing would lead to a few weeks later.

Paul had been scheduled to travel to Indonesia to minister to CMA missionaries at their annual field forum in Indonesia that summer—something that had been understandably overlooked on his calendar in the aftermath of his sudden death. The urgent call from the CMA office was a request that I go in Paul's place to speak and minister to the missionaries, who would be gathering in Irian Jaya in just a couple of weeks. Since Paul had been a good friend, I felt compelled to accept the request, and with the concurrence of my elder board chairman (and the church treasurer!), I agreed to take Paul's place.

I was briefed on the turbulent situation in Indonesia and reminded that the Indonesia team was in rough shape. Almost all of the fifty plus missionaries had been through six traumatic months on the field. Many of them had been evacuated during an armed insurrection across the archipelago. Now I was asked to go and minister to them. What was I going to say? What word did I have for them? How could I possibly minister to them in the midst of crisis?

My mind flashed back two years to a pastors' conference in Addis Ababa, Ethiopia, where I had been the speaker. Ethiopia had just emerged from a cruel and destructive seventeen-year Communist reign. Literally every one of the two hundred conference attendees had served some time in prison during the Communist siege. I was able to teach them some Bible and theology, but I recalled feeling so inadequate to teach them about the journey of faith. They had so much to teach me about life and death—and about negotiating life's turbulent waters.

It was just a few days after the call that I was arrested. No handcuffs or reading me my rights, but nearly as dramatic and, for me, life changing. I was sitting in my office, literally, just minding my own homiletic business, preparing a Communion message for the following Sunday. When I read John 13, I was arrested by something I had read a hundred times before! I had mentally just skimmed over it all those other times, because it was, after all, introductory. But this time the words seized my attention in a way it had never been before or since: "It was just before the Passover Feast. Jesus knew that the time had come for him to leave this world and go to the Father. Having loved his own who were in the world, he now showed them the full extent of his love. The evening meal was being served, and the devil had already prompted Judas Iscariot, son of Simon, to betray Jesus. *Jesus knew that the Father had put all things under his power, and that he had come from God and was returning to God*" (vv. 1–3, emphasis added).

Verse 3 took me prisoner that day and opened up for me one of the most remarkable passages of all Scripture: John 13–16, called the Upper Room Discourse or the Farewell Discourse. I soon discovered that other than the standard commentaries, there was almost nothing written about the Farewell Discourse. Don Carson's small volume *The Farewell Discourse and Final Prayer of Jesus* (Baker Book House, 1980) was the only thing I could find, in contrast to the numerous books written on the Sermon on the Mount or Jesus' prophetic sermon, the Olivet Discourse.

As I continued to focus on John 13:3 at the start of the farewell discourse, I could not help but also be seized by John 16:33: "I have told you these things, so that in me you may have peace. In this world you will have trouble. But take heart! I have overcome the world." Somehow I realized that between these two bookends of this remarkable portion of Scripture was an answer to my question, What do I say to these people who are in a crisis?

As a pastor for nearly thirty years, I have always felt inadequate in those times of crisis that every pastor faces. I recall the times I drove in my car to intervene in the crisis of a family, praying, *Lord, what can I say to this family? Lord, what can I do that will make a difference? Lord, help me! I am in over my head on this one. Jesus, when you said, "Take heart!" that sounds so full of promise. When I say it, it sounds so empty.*

Crises come in various shapes and sizes. In my world they never seem to let up. Though I am no longer shepherding a congregation, hardly a day goes by that a friend or colleague is not suddenly thrust into a crisis of some kind—loss of a child, loss of a job, a critical health issue, a broken marriage, or some major injustice.

Sometimes it is the Valley of Baca (Psalm 84:6, "valley of tears"). Sometimes it is the valley of the shadow of death (Psalm 23:4). It is Jesus who told us, "Take heart" (John 16:33). Perhaps that is why Christians call Jesus the lily of the *valleys* (from Song of Songs 2:1)—not the lily of the valley. He is with us in all the valleys, and he wants us to learn from his words and his example how to master our crises in life. In John 13–16, as I began to see, Scripture provides an inviting portrait of Jesus, the lily of the valleys, who wants to coach us through times of crisis. Jesus spoke to his disciples on the eve of the greatest personal crisis anyone could possibly imagine, as the forces of hell were unleashed on the God-Man. Yet we see Jesus this night—as always—in possession of complete health, mentally, emotionally, and spiritually. Not only was he well prepared for the moment, he used the evening to coach his disciples on navigating the storm they were facing on *their* journey.

The lessons I drew from John 13–16 so clearly ministered to the needs of the CMA missionaries in Indonesia that I continued to teach from this arresting portion of God's Word over the following few years to missionaries in France, the Middle East, Argentina, and finally in the Philippines. God's Word spoke to people in times of crisis in profound ways. After some years of presenting these insights in various setting around the world, I have been encouraged to render them into book form. As I pulled together a very rough first draft, I felt at times as if I was trying to scoop water out of the ocean with my hands in order to fill a pail, knowing that while there is more than enough water to overflow the pail, my cupped yet leaky hands are inadequate for the task. After all, who am I to presume to write about such things? What do I really know about hardship and suffering and crisis? Most of my difficult seasons have been like a few passing clouds compared to the dark thunderstorms that have ruined others' lives. To paraphrase Paul, my light and momentary suffering has been nothing compared with what others have passed through.

Then at the end of 2005, not long after I roughed out a first draft, I was diagnosed with an incurable lung disease, *sarcoidosis*, which had already advanced to stage four (*interstitial pulmonary fibrosis*) by the time it was diagnosed. My life changed. My job as vice president of the National Association of Evangelicals came to an end. I went on disability. My wife went back to work full time while I went on oxygen full time. While a barrage of medications helps to slow the advance of the disease, short of divine healing I am dying.

Sometime later, as I began to review the lessons I had sketched out in my rough draft from the farewell discourse, I realized that the truths I had taught others began ministering to my spirit in ways I could not have imagined. So this is no academic treatise for me. I am in a life-and-death crisis of my own. The insights in this book are not so much lessons from my journey but lessons *for* my journey. These truths gathered from God's Word that have been a great encouragement to others now encourage me.

Navigating Your Perfect Storm explores how Jesus—on the threshold of his unprecedented and unparalleled life crisis—prepared his disciples for the crises that he promised his followers would encounter on their spiritual journeys. This book is drawn from John's account—his seminar notes, if you will, missing from the other Gospels—from Jesus' crash course on survival skills on the night before he died. John 13–16 not only records for us the events of that evening but also offers a remarkable profile of one who is mentally, emotionally, and spiritually prepared for the cosmic conflict we call Good Friday. He had come to the fulcrum of his earthly life (and more important, the pivotal moment of all human history), and he had come as fully prepared as one can be. Yet in the face of his own crisis, Jesus used his last meal with his disciples to equip them for the inevitable life crises they would face as his followers.

Navigating Your Perfect Storm begins by setting the background for the Last Supper and the "seminar" that accompanied it. Jesus had prepared for this moment through a lifetime of events—including the critical temptations in the wilderness—by which he had learned the spiritual disciplines he needed to master. Those lessons included not only learning the supremacy of the spirit over the flesh but also extended to resisting the temptation to call on the myriads of angels at his disposal.

Navigating Your Perfect Storm is not a series of sermons or a how-to self-help book but a set of reflections, insights, and illustrations—based on the "seminar notes" John took on our behalf—for those who seek to follow Jesus today. As our world increasingly crumbles, Jesus offers peace for those who will deploy his anchors and heed his admonitions.

Dr. Bob Wenz
Colorado Springs
August 2009

The Farewell Discourse
John 13–16

It was just before the Passover Feast. Jesus knew that the time had come for him to leave this world and go to the Father. Having loved his own who were in the world, he now showed them the full extent of his love.

The evening meal was being served, and the devil had already prompted Judas Iscariot, son of Simon, to betray Jesus. Jesus knew that the Father had put all things under his power, and that he had come from God and was returning to God; so he got up from the meal, took off his outer clothing, and wrapped a towel around his waist. After that, he poured water into a basin and began to wash his disciples' feet, drying them with the towel that was wrapped around him.

He came to Simon Peter, who said to him, "Lord, are you going to wash my feet?"

Jesus replied, "You do not realize now what I am doing, but later you will understand."

"No," said Peter, "you shall never wash my feet."

Jesus answered, "Unless I wash you, you have no part with me."

"Then, Lord," Simon Peter replied, "not just my feet but my hands and my head as well!"

Jesus answered, "A person who has had a bath needs only to wash his feet; his whole body is clean. And you are clean, though not every one of you." For he knew who was going to betray him, and that was why he said not every one was clean.

When he had finished washing their feet, he put on his clothes and returned to his place. "Do you understand what I have done for you?" he asked them. "You call me 'Teacher' and 'Lord,' and rightly so, for that is what I am. Now that I, your Lord and Teacher, have washed your feet, you also should wash one another's feet. I have set you an example that you should do as I have done for you. I tell you the truth, no servant is greater than his master, nor is a messenger greater than the one who sent him. Now that you know these things, you will be blessed if you do them.

"I am not referring to all of you; I know those I have chosen. But this is to fulfill the scripture: 'He who shares my bread has lifted up his heel against me.'

"I am telling you now before it happens, so that when it does happen you will believe that I am He. I tell you the truth, whoever accepts anyone I send accepts me; and whoever accepts me accepts the one who sent me."

After he had said this, Jesus was troubled in spirit and testified, "I tell you the truth, one of you is going to betray me."

His disciples stared at one another, at a loss to know which of them he meant. One of them, the disciple whom Jesus loved, was re-clining next to him. Simon Peter motioned to this disciple and said, "Ask him which one he means."

Leaning back against Jesus, he asked him, "Lord, who is it?"

Jesus answered, "It is the one to whom I will give this piece of bread when I have dipped it in the dish." Then, dipping the piece of bread, he gave it to Judas Iscariot, son of Simon. As soon as Judas took the bread, Satan entered into him.

"What you are about to do, do quickly," Jesus told him, but no one at the meal understood why Jesus said this to him. Since Judas had charge of the money, some thought Jesus was telling him to buy what was needed for the Feast, or to give something to the poor. As soon as Judas had taken the bread, he went out. And it was night.

When he was gone, Jesus said, "Now is the Son of Man glorified and God is glorified in him. If God is glorified in him, God will glorify the Son in himself, and will glorify him at once.

"My children, I will be with you only a little longer. You will look for me, and just as I told the Jews, so I tell you now: Where I am going, you cannot come.

"A new command I give you: Love one another. As I have loved you, so you must love one another. By this all men will know that you are my disciples, if you love one another."

Simon Peter asked him, "Lord, where are you going?"

Jesus replied, "Where I am going, you cannot follow now, but you will follow later."

Peter asked, "Lord, why can't I follow you now? I will lay down my life for you."

Then Jesus answered, "Will you really lay down your life for me? I tell you the truth, before the rooster crows, you will disown me three times!

"Do not let your hearts be troubled. Trust in God; trust also in me. In my Father's house are many rooms; if it were not so, I would have told you. I am going there to prepare a place for you. And if I go and prepare a place for you, I will come back and take you to be with me that you also may be where I am. You know the way to the place where I am going."

Thomas said to him, "Lord, we don't know where you are going, so how can we know the way?"

Jesus answered, "I am the way and the truth and the life. No one comes to the Father except through me. If you really knew me, you would know my Father as well. From now on, you do know him and have seen him."

Philip said, "Lord, show us the Father and that will be enough for us."

Jesus answered: "Don't you know me, Philip, even after I have been among you such a long time? Anyone who has seen me has seen the Father. How can you say, 'Show us the Father'? Don't you believe that I am in the Father, and that the Father is in me? The words I say to you are not just my own. Rather, it is the Father, living in me, who is doing his work. Believe me when I say that I am in the Father and the Father is in me; or at least believe on the evidence of the miracles themselves. I tell you the truth, anyone who has faith in me will do what I have been doing. He will do even greater things than these, because I am going to the Father. And I will do whatever you ask in my name, so that the Son may bring glory to the Father. You may ask me for anything in my name, and I will do it.

"If you love me, you will obey what I command. And I will ask the Father, and he will give you another Counselor to be with you forever—the Spirit of truth. The world cannot accept him, because it neither sees him nor knows him. But you know him, for he lives with you and will be in you. I will not leave you as orphans; I will come to you. Before long, the world will not see me anymore, but you will see me. Because I live, you also will live. On that day you will realize that I am in my Father, and you are in me, and I am in you. Whoever has my commands and obeys them, he is the one who loves me. He who loves me will be loved by my Father, and I too will love him and show myself to him."

Then Judas (not Judas Iscariot) said, "But, Lord, why do you intend to show yourself to us and not to the world?"

Jesus replied, "If anyone loves me, he will obey my teaching. My Father will love him, and we will come to him and make our home with him. He who does not love me will not obey my teaching. These words you hear are not my own; they belong to the Father who sent me.

"All this I have spoken while still with you. But the Counselor, the Holy Spirit, whom the Father will send in my name, will teach you all things and will remind you of everything I have said to you. Peace I leave with you; my peace I give you. I do not give to you as the world gives. Do not let your hearts be troubled and do not be afraid.

"You heard me say, 'I am going away and I am coming back to you.' If you loved me, you would be glad that I am going to the Father, for the Father is greater than I. I have told you now before it happens, so that when it does happen you will believe. I will not speak with you much longer, for the prince of this world is coming. He has no hold on me, but the world must learn that I love the Father and that I do exactly what my Father has commanded me.

"Come now; let us leave.

"I am the true vine, and my Father is the gardener. He cuts off every branch in me that bears no fruit, while every branch that does bear fruit he prunes so that it will be even more fruitful. You are already clean because of the word I have spoken to you. Remain in me, and I will remain in you. No branch can bear fruit by itself; it must remain in the vine. Neither can you bear fruit unless you remain in me.

"I am the vine; you are the branches. If a man remains in me and I in him, he will bear much fruit; apart from me you can do nothing. If anyone does not remain in me, he is like a branch that is thrown away and withers; such branches are picked up, thrown into the fire and burned. If you remain in me and my words remain in you, ask whatever you wish, and it will be given you. This is to my Father's glory, that you bear much fruit, showing yourselves to be my disciples.

"As the Father has loved me, so have I loved you. Now remain in my love. If you obey my commands, you will remain in my love, just as I have obeyed my Father's commands and remain in his love.

I have told you this so that my joy may be in you and that your joy may be complete. My command is this: Love each other as I have loved you. Greater love has no one than this, that he lay down his life for his friends. You are my friends if you do what I command. I no longer call you servants, because a servant does not know his master's business. Instead, I have called you friends, for everything that I learned from my Father I have made known to you. You did not choose me, but I chose you and appointed you to go and bear fruit—fruit that will last. Then the Father will give you whatever you ask in my name. This is my command: Love each other.

"If the world hates you, keep in mind that it hated me first. If you belonged to the world, it would love you as its own. As it is, you do not belong to the world, but I have chosen you out of the world. That is why the world hates you. Remember the words I spoke to you: 'No servant is greater than his master.' If they persecuted me, they will persecute you also. If they obeyed my teaching, they will obey yours also. They will treat you this way because of my name, for they do not know the One who sent me. If I had not come and spoken to them, they would not be guilty of sin. Now, however, they have no excuse for their sin. He who hates me hates my Father as well. If I had not done among them what no one else did, they would not be guilty of sin. But now they have seen these miracles, and yet they have hated both me and my Father. But this is to fulfill what is written in their Law: 'They hated me without reason.'

"When the Counselor comes, whom I will send to you from the Father, the Spirit of truth who goes out from the Father, he will testify about me. And you also must testify, for you have been with me from the beginning.

"All this I have told you so that you will not go astray. They will put you out of the synagogue; in fact, a time is coming when anyone who kills you will think he is offering a service to God. They will do such things because they have not known the Father or me. I have told you this, so that when the time comes you will remember that I warned you. I did not tell you this at first because I was with you.

"Now I am going to him who sent me, yet none of you asks me, 'Where are you going?' Because I have said these things, you are filled with grief. But I tell you the truth: It is for your good that I am going away. Unless I go away, the Counselor will not come to you; but if I go, I will send him to you. When he comes, he will convict the world of guilt in regard to sin and righteousness and judgment: in regard to sin, because men do not believe in me; in regard to righteousness, because I am going to the Father, where you can see me no longer; and in regard to judgment, because the prince of this world now stands condemned.

"I have much more to say to you, more than you can now bear. But when he, the Spirit of truth, comes, he will guide you into all truth. He will not speak on his own; he will speak only what he hears, and he will tell you what is yet to come. He will bring glory to me by taking from what is mine and making it known to you. All that belongs to the Father is mine. That is why I said the Spirit will take from what is mine and make it known to you.

"In a little while you will see me no more, and then after a little while you will see me."

Some of his disciples said to one another, "What does he mean by saying, 'In a little while you will see me no more, and then after a little while you will see me,' and 'Because I am going to the Father'?" They kept asking, "What does he mean by 'a little while'? We don't understand what he is saying."

Jesus saw that they wanted to ask him about this, so he said to them, "Are you asking one another what I meant when I said, 'In a little while you will see me no more, and then after a little while you will see me'? I tell you the truth, you will weep and mourn while the world rejoices. You will grieve, but your grief will turn to joy. A woman giving birth to a child has pain because her time has come;

but when her baby is born she forgets the anguish because of her joy that a child is born into the world. So with you: Now is your time of grief, but I will see you again and you will rejoice, and no one will take away your joy. In that day you will no longer ask me anything. I tell you the truth, my Father will give you whatever you ask in my name. Until now you have not asked for anything in my name. Ask and you will receive, and your joy will be complete.

"Though I have been speaking figuratively, a time is coming when I will no longer use this kind of language but will tell you plainly about my Father. In that day you will ask in my name. I am not saying that I will ask the Father on your behalf. No, the Father himself loves you because you have loved me and have believed that I came from God. I came from the Father and entered the world; now I am leaving the world and going back to the Father."

Then Jesus' disciples said, "Now you are speaking clearly and without figures of speech. Now we can see that you know all things and that you do not even need to have anyone ask you questions. This makes us believe that you came from God."

"You believe at last!" Jesus answered. "But a time is coming, and has come, when you will be scattered, each to his own home. You will leave me all alone. Yet I am not alone, for my Father is with me.

"I have told you these things, so that in me you may have peace. In this world you will have trouble. But take heart! I have overcome the world."

PART I

ANTICIPATION

1
OUR NEED FOR ANCHORS

IN THIS WORLD YOU WILL HAVE TROUBLE. BUT TAKE
HEART! I HAVE OVERCOME THE WORLD.

The events of the first decade of the twenty-first century suggest that this century might be either the most tumultuous decade in history . . . or perhaps the last decade of human history.

We have seen the global economy teeter on the precipice of total meltdown and a resulting instability and recession.

We regularly are alerted to possible global pandemics that threaten to overshadow AIDS, which is nothing less than the greatest natural disaster in human history.

A global food crisis will deepen before it improves. Mothers in Haiti at times resort to feeding their children mud cookies.

Malaria still kills more than a million people every year.

Recent events bring a chilling reminder that terrorism is not going away and may well increase beyond what we've witnessed in New York, Washington, Madrid, London, and Bali. President Mahmoud Ahmadinejad of Iran threatens the West with "chaos," believing that such chaos will usher in the Twelfth Imam (an Islamic messiah figure), the global dominance of Islam, and the end of human history.

The Taliban is so deeply entrenched we wonder if that movement can ever be contained. International jihad seeks nuclear weapons that feasibly could be placed in a small boat and sent up the Potomac or Hudson River. The prime ministers of Israel warn that such capacity may soon be a reality. Some see in these events an unprecedented global crisis that will bring the return of Christ, anticipated in both the Bible and Qur'an (although with vastly different scenarios!).

Recent population projections suggest that at current rates, Islam will be a majority in Europe by the middle of this century, a situation with astounding potential consequences.

Although we recognize that the individual chances of being killed by a terrorist are still less than being struck by lightning, the glut of information about increasing crises from twenty-four-hour news channels can cause us to shut down mentally and emotionally. Global statistics overwhelm us, yet there is a chilling truth to Joseph Stalin's claim that where one death becomes a tragedy, a million simply becomes a statistic.

It really doesn't make much difference which eschatology is correct. If Christ returns as the kingdom is extended to the whole earth (the amillennial view), it will not be without an enormous upheaval of some variety and with the "sword." Radical Islam will not go away quietly. Or if the premillennial view is correct and Jesus returns before, during, or after a great tribulation, the return of Christ will be marked by a time of great global crisis. In either case, most of us will have to face trials. The world is neither a healthy place nor a safe place to be.

As well insulated as most of us in North America are from the crises of AIDS and al Qaeda, we are not insulated from the myriad of personal crises that repeatedly send us to the book of Job. Economic crises in the United States have cost millions of people their jobs, retirement savings, and hope. Even if we have been spared seasons of great difficulty, we are all personally aware of real people who are facing a real crisis, people who are very aware right at this moment that life is difficult.

Crises usually come without warning.

KEDGING

In a time of relative tranquility and comfort during my childhood, I learned a song in church declaring that "My anchor holds and grips the Solid Rock."[1] Storms and anchors were foreign concepts to me—whether literal or figurative. But now years later I am all too familiar with the reality that the storms of life come sweeping over you. Along my journey a few Navy veterans have been more than happy to teach me a thing or two about ships' anchors in days past. Anchors, they told me, were utilized in ports at anchorage and in times of storms—and, they added, anchors were also deployed when the waters were calm. And so they introduced me to the ancient art of kedging.

Kedging consisted of placing small *kedge* anchors into small boats and then rowing them out up to one-quarter mile, dropping those anchors in the water, and pulling the ship forward using the anchor capstan. Then the whole process was repeated. And repeated again. And again. Although the kedge anchors were most often used to pull a ship into a narrow anchorage, they were most cleverly deployed on windless days.

"Old Ironsides"—the USS *Constitution*—is the legendary American ship from the War of 1812, known best for deflecting British cannonballs from its wooden sides as though they were made of iron. Old Ironsides is also famous for escaping the British while outnumbered in a sea battle known in naval history as The Great Chase. A British squadron pursued the ship during a two-day period with almost no wind. American ingenuity yielded the method of self-propulsion called kedging, a practice that enabled the American ship to evade the British flotilla.

Of course, kedging is only a curious historical footnote, as even the great sailing ships that remain in service now have engines for negotiating ports and windless days. Yet I would invite you to join me in learning about spiritual kedging. This life skill has great promise that all of us should master, not for navigation of the seas but for the navigation of the soul through life. The seas of life are almost never calm, and we will find kedging a useful skill when the seas of life are stormy and we are looking for a safe harbor.

Life kedging involves dropping our anchors at the right places and allowing them to pull us forward through life, both through the winds and waves as well as the calmer days. Navigating life this way depends almost entirely on our willingness to acknowledge that we are otherwise adrift. Where we lower the kedges makes all the difference.

These anchors we set will pull us through life, moving us along day by day. They also keep us from drifting and crashing onto the rocks when the storms of life rage against our soul. I believe you will find that kedging is a life skill that all of us can master, learned not from a salty metaphor but from the remarkable and practical example of Jesus, who mastered the use of spiritual kedging in his own life and taught it to his disciples that last night.

While I would never presume to play pop psychologist or attempt to psychoanalyze Jesus of Nazareth, the way he navigated the storms of his own life—and in particular the greatest storm of his passion—serves as an invaluable model for those of us still at sea. Christ followers can hardly imagine a more trying time in any person's life than what Jesus passed through. It is little wonder that John devoted nearly half of his Gospel to an account of the last seven days of Jesus' life—when the sunshine of his celebrated arrival into Jerusalem gave little hint that the darkest storm clouds ever seen or experienced by the human soul were gathering in hell, preparing for that moment yet unseen. In his final week we see Jesus weeping over the city because its residents did not know the hour of their visitation—a unique moment when God came to judge and save the city. We see him eluding the Jewish leaders, escaping to Bethany each day. We read of repeated confrontations with his enemies at the temple, from the moment he arrived in the city and proceeded into the "den of robbers" (Matthew 21:13) with a makeshift whip. We read and attempt to decipher the prophetic sermon on the Mount of Olives regarding the destruction of the temple and Jesus' second advent. Always present through this week—as it had been for Jesus' entire life on earth—was a vivid mental picture in Jesus' mind of the cross and the excruciating (indeed, the word itself comes from "out of the cross") suffering he was to experience. Through it all he serves as our model, our navigator, our crisis coach. He entered into his own time of crisis with remarkable spiritual, emotional, and psychological health.

We know from the Gospels that the events of Jesus' last week came as no surprise to the Son of Man. Luke recorded that just after Peter's confession, or acknowledgment, that Jesus is the Christ, Jesus said, "The Son of Man must suffer many things and be rejected by the elders, chief priests and teachers of the law, and he must be killed and on the third day be raised to life" (Luke 9:22). Luke also clearly underscored Jesus' foreknowledge of the coming crucible when he noted, "As the time approached for him to be taken up to heaven, Jesus *resolutely* set out for Jerusalem" (Luke 9:51, emphasis added). It was, Jesus said, for *this hour* that he had come into the world.

Although Jesus was fully committed to doing God's will and drinking from the cup of suffering, his acceptance of God's will did not render his ordeal any less odious in any way. Indeed, it was so horrific a passage that he prayed the cup might be taken from him. Fortunately for us, in obedience to the Father and demonstrating untold maturity and fullness of character, Jesus was the one who took the deep breath and stepped forward into the crisis when he summoned his sleeping disciples, "Rise, let us go! Here comes my betrayer!" (Matthew 26:46).

We have a limited portrait of Jesus for the first thirty years of his life, before the commencement of his public ministry. Anne Rice's book on the childhood mind-set of Jesus daringly seeks to explore what we can only imagine—what Jesus as a toddler or a five-year-old comprehended.[2] But the Gospels tell us that as a young man at the significant age of twelve, Jesus was in the temple in Jerusalem engaged in a discussion of the Word of God. Although we do not have much in terms of detail, Luke tells us that "Jesus grew in wisdom and stature, and in favor with God and men" (2:52).

When we see Jesus beginning his public ministry at about age thirty, we see on display a thorough knowledge of both the Scriptures (that is, the Old Testament) and the massive volumes of the traditional commentaries of the Jews,[3] as revealed repeatedly in the Sermon on the Mount (Matthew 5, emphasis added):

> *You have heard that it was said to the people long ago,* "Do not murder, and anyone who murders will be subject to judgment." But I tell you . . .

> *You have heard that it was said,* "Do not commit adultery." But I tell you . . .

> *It has been said,* "Anyone who divorces his wife must give her a certificate of divorce." But I tell you . . .

> *Again, you have heard that it was said to the people long ago,* "Do not break your oath, but keep the oaths you have made to the Lord." But I tell you . . .

> *You have heard that it was said,* "Eye for eye, and tooth for tooth." But I tell you . . .

> *You have heard that it was said,* "Love your neighbor and hate your enemy." But I tell you . . .

The people had heard these teachings from the Mishnah, the accumulated commentaries and common understandings (and misunderstandings) of Scripture. Having mastered this body of texts, as well the Scriptures, Jesus was able to aptly respond to nearly every kind of circumstance. In his ministry, Jesus quoted directly or indirectly by allusion from every book of the Old Testament except for one (Esther). He did not live by bread alone, but by every word that proceeded from the mouth of God.

The discipline of prayer accompanied his study and mastery of the written Word. The Gospels are replete with accounts of Jesus in prayer. The night before he named his twelve first-tier disciples—including what must have been the agonizing selection of Judas—he spent the entire night in prayer. It was common for Jesus to go out to a solitary place before sunrise to pray. He often took some of his disciples with him to secluded places in the mountains to pray. So consistent was Jesus in his discipline of prayer that Judas would know precisely where to find him to betray him—in the garden of Gethsemane—because that is where Jesus regularly went to pray while in the city of Jerusalem.

THE MESSAGE OF JESUS IN PERSPECTIVE

We will discover that in addition to knowledge of the Word and a discipline of prayer, many other things contributed to the health of the one we look to for guidance. Before we move any further, however, we ought to consider how Jesus concluded his message, tying all these ideas together. "I have told you [all] these things, so that in me you may have peace. In this world you will have trouble. But take heart! I have overcome the world" (John 16:33).

In our world there is trouble, and there will be trouble. It is a normal part of life and a normal part of the Christian life as well. Long past are the days when a life of prosperity and without care was regarded as a sign of spirituality and God's special blessing. We ought not expect an exemption from difficulty while millions of faithful followers of Jesus—past, present, and future—have experienced, are experiencing, and will experience tribulation. If we are not experiencing tribulation right now, it may well come in the days ahead. It is part of living as followers of Jesus in a fallen and fragmenting world that is increasingly hostile toward him.

To this Jesus told us, "Take heart!" We can do that only because he has overcome the world and has given us a powerful model, important instruction, and essential equipment to enable us to navigate the tribulation we will encounter. He did not just wish his followers peace; he offered his peace—the same peace we see manifested in his life in the twelve hours following his final lesson. His desire, by his Word and by his Spirit, is to train us in spiritual kedging. He invites us to learn how to set anchors in our lives that will pull us through the storms that are still to come.

It is important to see where Jesus was going in his message. His major point—at the end of his classroom session—is also arresting by its candor and concise nature. The bulk of his evening discourse elaborated on how it is that we might take heart in a world full of trouble. In the end Jesus gave an exhortation and instructions for coping with the future tensions of life by looking to the past. Kedging through life's troubles depends on our confidence in what Jesus did in his earthly life: He lived in complete harmony with God, revealed the love of God by bearing our sin and brokenness on a cross, and gained the final victory over our great enemy, death, through his resurrection.

He admonished his followers to take heart because he had "overcome the world." I believe that the verb tense is significant. It is spoken in the past tense: he had already overcome the world. He had done so in a million small and large ways over the span of thirty-three years by living a life of perfect, sinless obedience to the Father. In conformity to the will of the Father, Jesus' life at every step was a preparation for this moment. He who was faithful in the little things would prove faithful in the big things.

I cannot endorse all that the late M. Scott Peck wrote in *The Road Less Traveled*, but his opening pages are breathtaking in their candor and comprehensive nature. He begins with a most remarkable three-word paragraph: "Life is difficult." Then he adds:

> What makes life difficult is that the process of confronting and solving problems is a painful one. . . . Indeed, it is *because* of the pain that events or conflicts engender in us that we call them problems. . . .
>
> Fearing the pain involved, almost all of us to a greater or lesser degree attempt to avoid problems. We procrastinate, hoping that they will go away. We ignore them, forget them, pretend they do not exist. We even take drugs to assist us in ignoring them so that deadening ourselves to the pain we can forget the problems that cause the pain. . . .
>
> This tendency to avoid problems and the emotional suffering inherent in them is the primary basis of all human mental illness. Since most of us have the tendency to a greater or lesser degree, most of us are mentally ill to a greater or lesser degree, lacking in complete mental health.[4]

It would be easy for me to argue with the assessment of this eminent psychiatrist that I am not mentally ill, but I must acknowledge that Peck is correct about me lacking complete mental health.

As we look at Jesus on the threshold of his great ordeal, did he not demonstrate what we all lack: complete mental health? That rigorous sanity can be seen in the Gospel accounts and especially in John 13–16, a section unique to this Gospel. As we review these chapters, we will focus on anchors to pull us through our trials and admonitions to keep us off the rocks.

I invite you to explore with me what Jesus told his disciples and what he modeled for them during his last night with them. They didn't grasp what was to happen in the next twenty-four hours, but Jesus did. Not only would he be put through an unimaginable crucible, but they would be "sifted as wheat" as well. Much of what we will learn comes from what is called the Farewell Discourse, but there is more; Jesus' words are only part of the story. This discourse is somewhat disjointed in that John gives us a summary, but one that is wide ranging and at the same time connected. The discourse can be segmented by highlighting Jesus' repeated phrases such as "I have told you this . . . ," but I have opted to seize upon five anchors and two admonitions that Jesus gives to all who draw near to him in their valleys.

2

PREPARING FOR
THE KAIROS MOMENT

I HAVE TOLD YOU THESE THINGS, SO THAT IN ME YOU
MAY HAVE PEACE. IN THIS WORLD YOU WILL HAVE
TROUBLE.

Would anyone object if I were to begin this chapter with "It
was the best of times; it was the worst of times" or "It was a
dark and stormy night"?[1] Which of these two clichés might you use
to describe your life at this time?

It was, in fact, the best of times and the worst of times, not in the
Roman outposts of London and Paris, but at the eastern backwater
of the empire, in Jerusalem, it was a dark and stormy night of the
soul. The time was the spring of AD 30 (or, using an equally valid
reconstruction, the spring of AD 33).[2] Jesus had come to Jerusalem
for the last time during his earthly life. This visit to the capital city
began with a clear statement of purpose, according to Luke, as we
noted in the previous chapter: "As the time approached for him to
be taken up to heaven, Jesus *resolutely* set out for Jerusalem" (Luke
9:51, emphasis added). Jesus had an appointment to keep on that
city's Mount Moriah—an appointment set on our behalf before the

foundation of the world, an appointment on which all human history hinges.

In some ways it was the best of times. Jesus entered the city on Monday[3] to a boisterous reception from thousands of pilgrims who had jammed Jerusalem for the Passover. The celebration that took place—where the stones would have been ordered to cry out had the crowds remained silent—belied the reality that Jesus had passed the zenith of his popularity some months before. In fact, Jesus announced and initiated this final journey to Jerusalem about the time the bubble of popularity had begun to burst. He had just fed the five thousand. The crowds, who were delighted with the prospect of a king who could feed them liberally, sought to make him king by force. Jesus had resisted them because he had not come to be a political ruler but a spiritual redeemer. Instead, Jesus began to teach the crowds some very radical truths about another kind of bread:

> Then Jesus declared, "I am the bread of life. He who comes to me will never go hungry, and he who believes in me will never be thirsty. But as I told you, you have seen me and still you do not believe. . . ."
>
> At this the Jews began to grumble about him because he said, "I am the bread that came down from heaven." They said, "Is this not Jesus, the son of Joseph, whose father and mother we know? How can he now say, 'I came down from heaven'?"
>
> "Stop grumbling among yourselves," Jesus answered. "No one can come to me unless the Father who sent me draws him, and I will raise him up at the last day. . . . I am the bread of life. Your forefathers ate the manna in the desert, yet they died. But here is the bread that comes down from heaven, which a man may eat and not die. I am the living bread that came down from heaven. If anyone eats of this bread, he will

live forever. This bread is my flesh, which I will give for the life of the world."

Then the Jews began to argue sharply among themselves, "How can this man give us his flesh to eat?"

Jesus said to them, "I tell you the truth, unless you eat the flesh of the Son of Man and drink his blood, you have no life in you. Whoever eats my flesh and drinks my blood has eternal life, and I will raise him up at the last day. For my flesh is real food and my blood is real drink. Whoever eats my flesh and drinks my blood remains in me, and I in him. Just as the living Father sent me and I live because of the Father, so the one who feeds on me will live because of me. This is the bread that came down from heaven. Your forefathers ate manna and died, but he who feeds on this bread will live forever." . . .

On hearing it, many of his disciples said, "This is a hard teaching. Who can accept it?" (John 6:35–36, 41–44, 48–58, 60).

Then John adds this most significant historical observation in verse 66: "From this time many of his disciples turned back and no longer followed him."

About the same time, this rabbi and his disciples were in Caesarea where Peter made his confession that Jesus was none other than "the Christ, the Son of the living God." During that conversation the disciples begrudgingly acknowledged that the crowds who followed Jesus had little or no solid understanding of who he was. Elijah said some; Jeremiah said others; John the Baptist said still others. The surveys of the crowds were uncertain and mixed. The Gospels then tell us that soon after this reading of the polls, Jesus announced for the first time to the Twelve that he was going to Jerusalem to be handed over to the Gentiles to be killed.

With the ovation that Jesus received on the road from Bethany into Jerusalem, this time appeared to be the best of times. But many of those who cheered "Hosanna!" that day were perhaps confused about who this really was. Perhaps some were previously followers who had later "turned back"—and yet they still held Jesus in high esteem. They did not believe or comprehend his radical message sufficiently to follow him. Certainly, the disciples thought this was the best of times. In spite of Jesus having prepared them over several months for the eventuality of his death and in spite of having a solid grasp of his identity, the disciples, as they worked their way to Jerusalem, clearly had not yet put the pieces together. (Recall that it was in Luke 9 that Jesus resolutely set out for Jerusalem—and this comment refers to a specific moment in time as much as eight months earlier.) Jesus' disciples, instead, were basking in the apparent popularity of their rabbi, unaware that the wheels were about to be ripped from their bandwagon.

Jesus, however, knew that it was to be the worst of times. The Gospels tell us that when the city came into sight, he wept over it. The word picture here is one of convulsively sobbing, even blubbering. It is the kind of crying that makes those around feel uncomfortable. He wept because no one in the city understood the *kairos* moment had arrived: "You did not recognize the *time* of God's coming to you" (Luke 19:44, emphasis added).

Two Greek words for time are used in the New Testament. *Chronos*—from which we get *chronological, chronometer, anachronism*—refers to sequential time (measured in hours, days, weeks, months, and years). *Kairos* refers to a specific moment or season in time.

Jesus wept because the pivotal *kairos* moment in history had arrived, and no one seemed to notice. Jesus had been to Jerusalem before, of course, but those visits were not "the right time." John's Gospel tells us clearly the difference between this Passover visit and the one made just a year before:

After this, Jesus went around in Galilee, purposely staying away from Judea because the Jews there were waiting to take his life. But when the Jewish Feast of Tabernacles was near, Jesus' brothers said to him, "You ought to leave here and go to Judea, so that your disciples may see the miracles you do. No one who wants to become a public figure acts in secret. Since you are doing these things, show yourself to the world." For even his own brothers did not believe in him.

Therefore Jesus told them, "The right time for me has not yet come; for you any time is right. The world cannot hate you, but it hates me because I testify that what it does is evil. You go to the Feast. I am not yet going up to this Feast, because for me the right time has not yet come." Having said this, he stayed in Galilee (John 7:1–9).

This moment was different, however; it was the right moment. It was the *kairos* moment of God's visitation to Jerusalem fulfilling the purpose and the promises of God. Sadly, the whole world would miss it when it happened.

Jesus was always conscious of the right time. Early in his ministry, some three years before, he allowed his mother, Mary, to put him on the spot at a wedding feast in Cana. However, he politely told her she really was intruding: "My time [kairos] has not yet come" (John 2:4). From this first public miracle through three years of public ministry, the Gospels tell us repeatedly things that happened and didn't happen because "his time had not yet come."

THE GROWING PLOT TO KILL JESUS

Even as the Jewish leaders wondered if Jesus would come to Jerusalem for the Passover, they had already begun to plot together to take his life. Tension in the city was high and getting higher.

Although there was deep suspicion and resentment toward Jesus for his teachings, what fomented the plot against him appears to have been much more a matter of business. At stake for the Jewish leaders was what they earnestly believed to be the survival of their primary industry: the temple. The high priest himself warned that if the "Jesus problem" was not dealt with, there was a great risk that the Romans would "come and take away . . . our place"—as in place of business.[4] The Jewish temple was the great central industry of the nation; it was the economic engine—the Microsoft of the whole economy of Israel. The temple and its ongoing mechanism of sacrifice was the greatest source of national revenue because people came from all over the Roman Empire to sacrifice at the temple during the high holy days. A vast tourism business that housed and fed thousands of pilgrim-tourists each year rippled out from the temple as well. The Passover was to Jerusalem what the Super Bowl is each year to its host city.

This was all seriously corrupted, of course. As pilgrims came to the temple at specific seasons to offer sacrifices, they were often told that sacrifices brought in from the provinces were certainly unacceptable to God because they no longer could be considered without blemish, having made the journey on the roads of ancient Israel. For God's altar, special sacrificial animals were provided (for a price) for faithful pilgrims who sang the songs of ascent as they climbed the steps of the temple: "Open for me the gates of righteousness; I will enter and give thanks to the LORD. This is the gate of the LORD through which the righteous may enter. I will give you thanks, for you answered me; you have become my salvation" (Psalm 118:19–21).

As they reached the highest steps of the temple courts, the pilgrims realized that these were hardly the gates of righteousness as they encountered the outrageous high prices. But they were likely reminded by the temple mafia of the price of the convenience of not having to bring their sacrifices with them. Here at the house of prayer for all nations, two doves no longer sold for a penny, as the markups reached extortion levels.

The business of the temple, we are told, was complicated further by the unfortunate problem of money. Roman coins with the likeness of Caesar certainly could not be used to purchase an acceptable sacrifice to God. Profane money had to be exchanged for temple currency (shekels), so temple management made sure arriving tourists could find a currency exchange nearby, just as at airports today. And just as at airport currency exchanges today, a surcharge was added, only much higher than the nominal 5 percent. How high? High enough that Jesus—on his first day in the city—burst into the "den of robbers," fashioned a whip from rope, drove out the money changers, and overturned their tables. The management of the temple, deeply concerned about their license to continue operating under Roman rule, did not take kindly to Jesus' incursion into the temple. The skirmish that resulted happened right under the noses of Roman soldiers stationed on the ramparts of the Antonia Fortress overlooking the temple precincts. The tension in the city—already high at this moment—went even higher as the Jewish leadership pondered their "Jesus problem."

ANTICIPATING WHAT THE KAIROS MOMENT WOULD BRING

Most of our crisis moments come unannounced, of course. Sometimes I can look back and think I might have possibly seen or should have seen something coming. For Jesus, however, this Passover season would bring a *kairos* moment that he had long anticipated. Jesus knew clearly and precisely what time it was, as well as its portent. The specter of a Roman cross must have been burned into his mind. The whole gruesome process of crucifixion, invented by the Assyrians, was carried out with regularity, if not relish, by the Romans for the specific purpose of fixing the image into the minds of all its subjected people and nations. Slave revolts, such as that led by Spartacus, ended with the crucifixion of hundreds of slaves along major thoroughfares so that everyone could see and remember the horror that awaited those who challenged the authority or tarnished the glory of Rome. Jesus, growing up in an occupied Roman province, had certainly witnessed the cruelty of crucifixion some time during his life. Perhaps many times.

When *The Passion of the Christ* came to movie screens in 2003, it quickly differentiated itself from any of the earlier Hollywood versions of the crucifixion. Here we saw Jesus beaten beyond recognition and then crucified with ropes pulling his arms to stretch them out taut and hold them in place for the executioner. It was a ghastly vision for most of us; I recall moments when I turned my head away and wept. Yet almost every inhabitant of the Roman Empire saw crucifixions up close. Unlike lambs silent before the slaughter, most of those executed in that brutal manner filled the air with cries of pain and fear. The Roman government not did give crucifixion an R rating or limit viewing to adults after the children went to bed. Rome wanted people of all ages to see and hear crucifixions because these executions served a vital role in Rome's program for controlling the population with terror.

Our faith as Christians centers on the horrific crucifixion of Jesus of Nazareth with all its pain, its humiliation, and its shame. For this reason and for this moment he had come into the world.[5] The apostle Paul wrote that he aspired to know nothing except Jesus and him crucified (1 Corinthians 2:2). Now, if Paul claimed to have lived intentionally with such a fully ripened and permeating knowledge of Jesus and him crucified (he certainly witnessed crucifixions and may have witnessed the crucifixion of Christ, although there is no direct evidence of this as there is for Paul's witnessing the stoning of Stephen), certainly something parallel might be said of Jesus. Jesus came to this *kairos* moment almost obsessively conscious, his mind permeated with the realization that he, the Lamb of God, would be crucified on a Roman cross on Friday morning at nine. He had lived with the knowledge of this *kairos* moment every day of his life. Now his moment had come.

Knowing that my lungs are filling up with scar tissue day by day, no day passes that I do not process in some way—generally a healthy way—some thoughts about death. Forty-three years have passed since I watched my father, Harry, die of cancer over a very short interval of time. The memories are still vivid. He was only fifty-two and suffered from cancer in an era when doctors opened patients up on the operating table, took one look, closed patients back up, and sent them home to die. He was a believer, but he never shared any of his journey with his children; therefore, I really don't know how he processed all this in his heart and mind. Now as I deal with a terminal illness—although with no date circled on the calendar—I am beginning to understand that it is a lonely journey that others cannot fully understand.

I also have reflected on my experiences as a pastor for more than twenty-five years as I watched others die from terminal illnesses and witnessed a variety of responses from doctors, families, and the patients themselves. I recall being asked not to tell a terminally ill person that he was dying because the family didn't want to upset him. I've seen families in denial. I've seen remarkable expressions of hope in heaven. I feel like I've seen it all. Yet it did not fully prepare me for being on the other side of the equation.

The residue of all these experiences remains in my mind as I contemplate what Jesus must have been thinking as the days of that week moved from Monday to Tuesday and inexorably and divinely toward that Friday morning appointment with a Roman cross. When I see a crisis coming, I tend to want to hide, but that reveals my lack of complete health. Jesus knew all his life this day was coming and he never flinched—that reveals his complete mental, emotional, and spiritual health.

Certainly Jesus was able to comfort himself with the knowledge of the final outcome. The book of Hebrews states that he "for the joy set before him endured the cross." There was the joy of knowing that by his death he would purchase "men for God from every tribe and language and people and nation" (Revelation 5:9). There was also the joy of knowing he had done the Father's will, the joy of victory over Satan, the joy of resurrection, and the return to the glory of heaven—these were all part of the joy set before him. But the Word tells us that he still had to endure the cross. No minor crucible, no minor victory here. This was the anchor that pulled the Savior through his sacrificial death.

As I cope with the inexorable realities of pulmonary fibrosis, on some days I wish I knew how many years or perhaps months I have left. Some days I don't want to know; I just want to live my life. I wonder how I would react if God were to actually reveal the exact number of my days. How would I process it emotionally if the number were small? Or larger than I thought? I appreciate the wisdom of Ravi Zacharias, who noted simply that each year as we age, each day represents a greater portion of our remaining life than the year, or even the day, before.[6]

We might not wish to know what the future holds if it is traumatic. So in Jesus' case, consciously knowing every day of his life the exact time and circumstances of his violent beating and death on a cross must have represented a significant burden. Some people today, with diagnoses of cancer or ALS (Lou Gehrig's disease) or another terminal illness, opt to end their lives rather than face what is likely to unfold. It is evidence of Jesus' psychological and spiritual health that he was able to live the thirty-some years of his life knowing the *kairos* to come. As much as we might want to know the details of the future, we are not really psychologically healthy enough to handle such information. Jesus was.

On Thursday night of that week, Jesus shared a final meal with his disciples, washed their feet, and taught them one last time. He taught about tribulation: "In this world you will have trouble." The Greek word in the original manuscript is *thlipsis*, which is generally translated "tribulation." It can refer to trouble in the general sense as well as the more specific biblical reference to "the time of trouble for Jacob"—the tribulation of Revelation. *Thlipsis* refers to the severe practice in antiquity during which, to extract information or to gain a confession, a man was placed on the ground and weights were placed on top of him. More and more weight was added as his frame was crushed and he gasped to breathe. Historically noted as an agonizing punishment, it was not uncommon for a man to be crushed to death this way, which in many cases was the practitioners' intent.[7]

As he met with the disciples for what he knew was his final meal with them, Jesus sought to coach them—by word and the example of his own life—how to encounter the *kairos* moments in their lives when tribulations come. He sought to provide them kedges to pull them through the tribulation coming into their lives, not only that night but also for the weeks and months and years to come. What was true for Peter must have been true for others, if not all of them: "Satan has asked to sift you as wheat" (Luke 22:31). Satan did sift Peter that night as he denied Christ three times. The apostle James would face a crisis at the hands of Herod just a short time after Pentecost. Peter would receive another shake at the hand of Herod, who placed "the rock" in prison, a prison from which God delivered him by a shaking of another kind. John, who recorded for us the events of that evening in his Gospel, would face his tribulation on the Island of Patmos, perhaps sixty years later. Knowing this, Jesus was eager to prepare his disciples to pass triumphantly through their tribulations. So he prayed that their faith would not fail and also instructed and equipped them to that end.

Because Jesus was not only addressing the Eleven but all who would follow him, I believe it is incumbent on me and every Christ follower to be prepared for and even anticipate that there will be *thlipsis*. James 1 tells us not to be surprised when it comes, and even to welcome these trials. Therefore, if *thlipsis* of some kind is going to be part of my life, I want to understand better how Jesus endured the great crisis in his life—the abandonment by his friends, the betrayal by Judas, the injustice of sham trials, the beatings and scourging, the mockery, the humiliation, and finally the cross. While some Christians have lived wonderful, seemingly untroubled lives and died quietly and peacefully of old age, none of us has such a guarantee and only a few of us will experience such a trajectory. I want to know better how Jesus was able to endure his great personal crisis because we are also called to endure, and I don't know what I might yet face in the future.

You and I will not face a Roman cross, but Hebrews 11 reminds us that followers of Jesus have throughout history endured a whole litany of suffering for the sake of following him faithfully: "Others were tortured and refused to be released, so that they might gain a better resurrection. Some faced jeers and flogging, while still others were chained and put in prison. They were stoned; they were sawed in two; they were put to death by the sword. They went about in sheepskins and goatskins, destitute, persecuted and mistreated—the world was not worthy of them."

There is little doubt that tribulation is the defining characteristic of the lives of many Christians, even as I write this. It is estimated that as many as a hundred thousand followers of Jesus Christ around the world will be killed for their faithful witness in a typical year. For them and for millions more at risk each day, Jesus' declaration that "in this world you will have trouble" takes on far more meaning and immediacy than it does for those of us in North America. Although efforts to restrict religious freedom in the United States are the work of the same serpent who brings about the martyrdom of Christians in Indonesia, it is more often the rattle end of that snake that North

Americans deal with than the fangs. Sadly, the North American church's limited response each November to the International Day of Prayer for the Persecuted Church suggests a denial or ignorance of the reality of rampant global tribulation today. Perhaps some have made the dangerous and mistaken conclusion that Jesus' declaration did not extend to us in the United States.

The ascendancy in late 2005 of an ultraradical Islamic president of Iran and his unbridled pursuit of nuclear weapons gives many pause. According to one Shia version of eschatology (Iran is overwhelmingly Shia although Shiites constitute only 10 percent of Islam), history will come to an end with the rise of the Twelfth Imam or *Mahdi*, who is regarded as Islam's messiah. The Mahdi in Islamic eschatology is the prophesied redeemer of Islam who will change the world into a perfect Islamic society before *Yaum al-Qiyamah* (literally, "Day of the Resurrection"). The idea of a man who would arise to right the injustices in the world of Islam is now widely held, however. The Mahdi, according to majority Sunni and Shiite traditions, will arise at some point before the day of judgment, institute a kingdom of justice, and will in the last days fight alongside a returned Jesus against the *Dajjal* (antichrist or false messiah). He will ascend after a season of chaos on the earth (a season of seven years) and then bring the world into submission to Allah.

Mahmoud Ahmadinejad has expressed his intent of fomenting such chaos on the earth in order to usher in the Mahdi. The Mahdi is said to be joined by Jesus (who never died) at Mecca. The Mahdi will instruct the restored prophet Jesus to pray properly, and Jesus will then instruct his mistaken followers to acknowledge and submit to Allah and Mohammed as his prophet. Ralph Stice, in his gripping study of Islamic eschatology, *From 9/11 to 666*, presents a sobering case for the rise of an Islamic antichrist within the next twenty years. Even secular news commentators are beginning to connect the dots: "Men like Ahmadinejad are no mystery. They are awake at the apocalypse. . . . What are we to make of [his] millenarianism belief expressed in the return of the Hidden Imam, the apocalyptic moment in history when the wicked are punished and the lowly inherit the earth? . . . What is one to make of the man's threat to 'wipe Israel off the map'?"[8]

Ahmadinejad and his circle are in an apocalyptic mood. The use of nuclear weapons would not bother them,[9] and now Iran claims to have nuclear capability.

We can argue about eschatology, but as I hinted earlier, the future may bring a time of great upheaval (or tribulation) for the church, regardless of how we read Daniel and Revelation. That upheaval might be the cost of taking the gospel to the nations as the kingdom of God is ushered in. There are rumors (and only that for now) of millions of Chinese believers who are preparing to take the gospel west along the old Silk Route of Asia—across the heart of the Arab Islamic world—realizing that most, if not all, will die for their witness for Christ. There might, alternatively, be a seventieth week of Daniel's trouble—the great tribulation—through which the church might pass.[10] Who of us can be so certain of our eschatology as to shrug off at least the possibility?

If a pretribulation rapture of the church delivers us, we might still face a major life crisis, even if it is only of the personal variety, as I have become aware in my own *kairos* moment. I want to be prepared for either. I hope Tim LaHaye and Jerry Jenkins, along with all my dispensational friends, are correct and that God will not let his church go through the great tribulation. I really hope they are right! But should God allow the church to pass through the tribulation yet spare the church from wrath, I would rather be prepared for that and help others to be prepared also. In either eventuality, we need Jesus to prepare us and equip us to navigate this crisis should that day come in our lifetime.

As we continue to read John's account of the Last Supper, it is as if we together sit in the corner of the upper room where Jesus shared his final meal with his disciples. We hear Jesus model and teach the character traits in his life that would take him through the darkest eighteen hours anyone could ever face. He equipped them for a crisis that would begin to unfold in the hours ahead and would enfold them as well. He had prepared his whole life for this *kairos* moment, and he wanted to make sure that he passed on to the Eleven the kedging anchors and admonitions that would prepare them for theirs. These anchors, which the Son of Man had set in his own life, were kedges that would enable him to pass through the violent storm of body and soul he was about to enter. Let's consider together how Jesus prepared for his tribulation.

THE MENTOR WHO LEARNED THE HARD WAY—THE RIGHT WAY

We don't know how many times the devil personally came to tempt and test Jesus, but the Gospel writers tell us that following the three temptations in the wilderness, the devil left him "until an opportune time" (Luke 4:13). It should be noted that Jesus' temptations came from demonic spirits rather than from his own heart, while many temptations we face come straight from our own hearts. While Jesus' temptations were certainly as real as, and even more intense than, those most of us have ever faced, he never yielded to a temptation, always enduring the full fury of it. The book of Hebrews is unequivocal that he was "tempted in every way, just as we are—yet was without sin."

There is much to learn from the three temptations recorded in Luke 4. Of course, there are numerous volumes written on the temptations of Christ, but my purpose is to just barely reference this portion of the Gospels.

Jesus was led into the wilderness from his baptism, having been filled with the Holy Spirit. This is a difficult concept to get our minds around because it is difficult to contemplate how the incarnate God-Man could ever be less than filled with the Spirit. Nevertheless, Luke clearly wanted to convey the importance of the fullness of the Spirit for the spiritual warfare that was about to commence. Jesus had come to the wilderness for forty days to learn obedience. The forty days were symbolic of Israel, the people who went into the wilderness for forty years of testing because they had failed to learn obedience. Whereas in the wilderness the anointed nation failed, Jesus the anointed Son (with the fullness of the Holy Spirit) would prevail.

The Gospels tell us that after forty days of fasting, Jesus was hungry. It is easy to miss the significance of this because we naively think, *Of course he was hungry; he hadn't eaten in forty days.* But that is not quite complete and therefore not quite accurate. Hunger accompanies fasting only for the first few days. After these first days there are no significant hunger pangs. This second phase of fasting lasts for a number of days based on the amount of reserves (fat) with which a person began the fast. On whatever day the reserves are depleted, the final phase of fasting commences. The body begins to feed on itself to sustain life—the person without food is beginning to die. At this time, hunger returns as the body gives one final desperate cry for food in order to avert death. Jesus, we are told, was hungry. Not only was he experiencing hunger, his body was desperate for food.

Satan tempted Jesus to turn stones into bread. Certainly there was no sin in turning stones into bread, and it would have been no sin for Jesus to eat. Yet he rebuked the tempter and resisted this temptation in order to demonstrate to Satan and to confirm in his own physical being that the spiritual realm is of higher priority than the fleshly realm. What is eternal is more important than what is temporal. The unseen is a higher reality than what is seen. Jesus would later say with a clear track record of his own experience: "The Spirit gives life; *the flesh counts for nothing*" (John 6:63, emphasis added). It might well be that when the author of Hebrews wrote that Jesus "learned obedience from what he suffered," he was referring in great part—if not in whole—to this temptation. Here in the wilderness Jesus learned the complete subjugation of the flesh to the spirit—the very discipline he would need to be able to face his enemies rather than to run from Judas and those who came to arrest him.

Satan tempted Jesus a second time, this time with a vision of all the kingdoms of the earth, offering them to Jesus in exchange for worship. Note two things with me at this juncture: First, the prince of this world certainly had the prerogative to offer this world to Jesus—it was his. Second, the prince of this world had wanted nothing more earnestly since his creation than that the King of Kings and Lord of Lords would bow before him in worship.

So the con game with Satan, always the same, began: trade with me on impulse for something with immediate appeal, something of lesser value. The "kingdoms of this world and their splendor" are at first glance rather appealing. But they were and remain part of this world, meaning that beneath the polished exterior we find all the sin and sorrow and suffering and sickness inherent in a fallen world. Not only did Satan offer Jesus damaged goods, but I believe both he and Jesus also knew that ultimately the kingdom of the world would become "the kingdom of our Lord and of his Christ" (Revelation 11:15). All the kingdoms of this world and the earth itself would be reclaimed and restored by God. The title to them would revert to the original owner. At one time in the past, the kingdom of heaven and the kingdom of this world were one. Although the rebellion of Satan prompted God to cede to him control of this world, the kingdom of heaven and the kingdom of earth shall be made one again and be made whole again.

The cost of this reconciliation was the cross and redemption of the fallen race of Adam. Satan sought to trick Jesus into taking the kingdoms of the earth without redeeming the lost and condemned sons of Adam. Jesus came to redeem people for God—not earthly kingdoms. The appeal of the offer was real—receive back the kingdoms of this world without having to redeem the lost race of Adam, without having to go through the suffering of the cross. Satan would have been delighted to make the trade.

Jesus rejected the offer and solidified the resolve within himself that he would take no shortcuts, however expedient they might be. The price—worshiping this fallen angel—was an unacceptable price to pay for anything Satan might offer, let alone property that would someday revert to the original owner. Here in the wilderness Jesus learned to stay the course and never take the path of least resistance, a discipline that he would need the night his enemies came for him with swords and clubs. He learned this aspect of obedience through suffering.

The third temptation required some untold mode of transport to the pinnacle of the temple. There Satan challenged Jesus to throw himself down, trusting that God would dispatch angels to catch him. The upside would be that all the thousands of people in the temple precincts would see Jesus' power over the forces of nature and be drawn to his miraculous display. Once again, Jesus was not taken in by the temptation; instead, he brought to a new level within himself the discipline he would need the night the high priests came to arrest him with an armed band. He would not call on angels to deliver him now at the pinnacle of the temple, nor would he call on them in the midst of his passion in surrender to the will of the Father.

You and I might not think of not calling on angels as one of the classic spiritual disciplines. At the cross, however, the Son of Man would need to have gained this spiritual discipline not to call on the twelve legions of angels (twelve thousand according to the Roman system) that the Father had put at his disposal. Jesus learned this spiritual discipline in the wilderness. As nails pierced his body, he would not call for the legions he knew were always standing by, swords drawn to defend the Prince of Glory.

THE IDENTITY OF OUR NAVIGATOR

More lessons come from the temptations of Christ in the wilderness than we have room for here. But please don't miss another of these, however. Satan prefaced each of these three temptations with the phrase "if you are the Son of God." It is a curious taunt by one who knew better than anyone whom he was talking to. In fact, if Jesus were not the Son of God, Satan would never have tested and tempted him at this point or in this way. (In chapter 3 we will look more closely at the important matter of Jesus' identity. And in chapter 4 we will hear from Jesus about how we can know who we are in him.) Identity was a critical matter in the wilderness for Jesus, and it can be a critical matter for us in our times in the wilderness. Although the temptation for us is not quite the same, Satan will readily test us on our certainty that we are children of God. A solid sense of identity is a primary anchor in the turbulence of life, perhaps our most important kedge. As we'll see, those issues of Jesus' identity were significant, but they were resolved long before he faced the great crisis in his life. There can be little doubt that as Jesus came to Jerusalem, he came prepared spiritually, emotionally, and psychologically. It was preparation that encompassed his whole life and included special times of preparation in the wilderness. He had systematically prepared his whole life for these few days and hours, the reason he came into the world.

Jesus, who was eager in the upper room to equip the Eleven for the storms that would rage against them, was himself fully equipped for the rage that would storm against him the next day at Golgotha. He was spiritually, emotionally, and psychologically as prepared as one can be—a model of health and a supplier of useful anchors and admonitions. He is our navigator in times of crisis. He was well anchored—and an able coach for those seeking to master kedging.

PART II
ANCHORS

3

ANCHOR 1:
LEARNING WHO WE ARE (PART 1)

JESUS KNEW THAT THE FATHER HAD PUT ALL THINGS
UNDER HIS POWER, AND THAT HE HAD COME FROM
GOD AND WAS RETURNING TO GOD.

John begins his review of this most important evening with a focus on the identity of Jesus. Jesus had gathered his disciples for what we call the Last Supper on what we believe to have been Thursday evening (traditionally called Maundy Thursday). John introduces his narrative account of this evening with a remarkable observation:

> It was just before the Passover Feast. Jesus knew that the time had come for him to leave this world and go to the Father. Having loved his own who were in the world, he now showed them the full extent of his love.
>
> The evening meal was being served, and the devil had already prompted Judas Iscariot, son of Simon, to betray Jesus. Jesus knew that the Father had put all things under his power, *and that he had come from*

God and was returning to God (John 13:1–3, emphasis added).

The first statement in John 13 that arrested my attention relates to Jesus identity: he knew that he had come from God and was returning to God.

The baby boomer generation, of which I am a part, has struggled mightily with the question, Who am I? A song written by Pete Townshend, fittingly of The Who, has been the theme song of *CSI*, one of television's most popular shows in recent years. Somewhere between punk and progressive, the song has the eerie sound and words the producer of CSI wanted: "Who are you? Who, who, who, who?" The words of the last verses bring some resolution to the endless series of interrogatories with surprising insights . . . that almost sound Christian.[1]

I was never a big fan of The Who, but "Who Are You?" struck a nerve in 1978 with a whole generation of young adults like me. Perhaps that is why more than one hundred songs with the same or a similar title are available for download to your iPod. Developmental psychologist Eric Erikson suggested that many of my generation developed a negative identity. In other words, boomers developed their identities in opposition to their antiheroes—people or groups of people they disliked and desired earnestly not to be like, especially parents.[2] These negative identities apparently proved to be unsatisfactory, because many of the marijuana-smoking protesters and rock musicians of the 1960s have ended up running for political office, heading up major corporations, consulting for the federal government on international terrorism, or even teaching at the universities they tried to shut down or burn down. Many of us boomers ended up trading in the what-I'm-against identity of the sixties and seventies for the what-I-do or what-I-own identity of the eighties and nineties.

Like many boomers, I struggled with the question of identity.

My difficulties were generational and gestational—I am an identical twin. I see identical twins from time to time and can only shake my head, knowing the hazards ahead for them as individuals. I cringe when I see occasional news features about national gatherings of dressed-alike adult identical twins. Often they reveal in interviews things that boggle my mind—such as that they married identical twins and live across the street from each other. That is a bit too much "twin-ness" for me because, while I have always had a good relationship with my brother, Richard, I didn't care for being a twin.

Being dressed alike was always uncomfortable. Fortunately we were never put in the same class at school. But the killer was my parents' friends' tendency to call both of us by the collective name BobbyDickie because they couldn't tell us apart. My parents, unfortunately, thought that moniker to be cute, so it persisted for years. The oft-repeated "Which one are you?" questions were of no help for an adolescent who was trying at a much deeper level to answer that very question. Later in this chapter I'll relate some of how that identity struggle resolved. It didn't happen overnight. In fact, I was nearly thirty before I had sufficiently worked through the issue. The process took a while, and John 13 was of enormous value.

We discover three important things regarding Jesus' identity in verse 3: first, Jesus knew the time had come. Second, Jesus knew that he had come from God and was returning to God. Third, Jesus knew that the Father had put all things under his authority. In the previous chapter we considered the importance of the first of these three— that Jesus knew the *kairos* time had come—so we will now move on to the second of these, that Jesus knew who he was.

DIVINE SELF-AWARENESS

Jesus knew that he had come from God and was returning to God. It is at first glance an obvious statement. Of course Jesus knew that he had come from God—he was the incarnate Son of God.

True enough. But I believe this statement, however obvious, is worth some significant further discussion because it gives insight into the whole issue of Jesus and his identity—an issue central to our faith. As we consider Jesus' identity—who he knew himself to be—we have to begin with the uniqueness of the identity issue for Jesus. If it is hard to clearly resolve the question of identity for an identical twin, how much more difficult must it be for one who is both fully God and fully man at the same time?

The history of Christology (the doctrine of who Jesus is) is one that has led some far from the truth of God's Word. Virtually every heresy that has plagued the church, from the first-century gnostics to today's neognostics like Elaine Pagels and Dan Brown, evolved from teachers who challenge (deny, denigrate, or distort) either the deity of Jesus, the humanity of Jesus, or the hypostatic union—the union between God and man in the person of Jesus—as taught clearly in the New Testament. Witness Lisa McLeod, quoted in the *Gwinnett Daily Post*, in the wake of *The Da Vinci Code*:

> To me, Jesus represents the human potential. To argue that he was just a man denies his divinity, and to say that he was solely divine ignores his humanity. In fact, I often wonder if the two conflicting views of Jesus—man or God—are convenient ways of letting us off the hook. If we believe he's God and no one can ever be as perfect as Jesus, why should we even try? And, if he was a mere mortal like the rest of us slobs, then perhaps there is no such thing as the divine.
>
> But, what if we embraced the idea that Jesus was both human and divine? It might mean that we are too. And we can no longer make any excuses for not acting like who we really are—MANIFESTATIONS of God on earth.
>
> Kind of scary, isn't it? Jesus symbolized the spark

of divinity in all of us. We don't need to know the
LITERAL truths of his life to understand and execute
the conceptual beauty of his message. He lived love
and he was killed by fear. What else do we really need
to know?[3]

I give my church history students a handout that catalogs eleven
heresies with off-putting names like Docetism, Nestorianism, and
Ebionitism. Each of them—from gnosticism of the first century to
Monophysitism in the seventh century, and all of the mutant offspring of these heresies propagated in the past thirteen centuries—
denies either that Jesus was fully God or denies that Jesus was fully
man. The major councils of the early church (such as those at Nicaea,
Constantinople, and Chalcedon) were in response to the various attacks on the orthodox teaching about Jesus as fully God and fully
man. The Nicene Creed, for example, was written in defense of the
doctrine of Christ as fully God and fully man:

> We believe in one God, the Father Almighty,
> Maker of heaven and earth, and of all things visible
>   and invisible.
> And in one Lord Jesus Christ, the only-begotten Son
>   of God,
> begotten of the Father before all worlds,
> God of God, Light of Light, very God of very God,
> begotten, not made, being of one substance with the
>   Father
> by whom all things were made. . . . [4]

The impact of the neognostic *Da Vinci Code* (both the book and
movie) continues to ripple through the church and culture. At
the heart of the novel, which many seemingly desire or wish to be
true, is the contention that it was not until the fourth century that
Constantine and the Council of Nicaea conspired to foist on the

empire the concept of the deity of Christ. Ignoring all the other errors in the book related to art and history, this fabrication is perhaps most easily and completely put aside by secular historical evidence. Correspondence dating from the late first century from Pliny the Younger (Gaius Plinius Caecilius Secundus), governor of Pontus-Bithynia, to Emperor Trajan, tells the emperor that Christians "recite a hymn among themselves to Christ, as though he were a god."[5] Paul's hymn in Philippians may in fact have been the song or one of the songs referred to by Pliny in his letter in volume ten of his correspondence. In this earliest extant hymn of the infant church, the focus is on the humanity and deity of Christ: "Who, being in very nature God, did not consider equality with God something to be grasped, but made himself nothing, taking the very nature of a servant, being made in human likeness. And being found in appearance as a man, he humbled himself and became obedient to death—even death on a cross!" (Philippians 2:6–8). To the church in Colossae Paul wrote that Jesus is "the image of the invisible God," and that "God was pleased to have all his fullness dwell in him." (Colossians 1:15, 19).

Paul's letters, with these two didactic portions to the early church, clearly articulate the biblical doctrine of Christ: He is God. Very God of Very God! He is also human, having been born of human flesh.

Even as we reaffirm the theological emphasis on the full humanity and full deity of Jesus, the more practical matter of what Jesus' psyche must have been like confronts us. We know that he was fully human, for he was tempted in every way but without sin (see Hebrews 4:15). For his temptations to have been real, Jesus' consciousness must have been fully human according to any definition. Because he had set aside his divine attributes of omnipresence and omniscience when he came and took on the human body that God had prepared for him (Hebrews 10:5), Jesus must have had a fully human consciousness like ours. We can only ponder and speculate how his absolute divinity manifested itself in his absolutely human consciousness. It is, in fact, the inability of some to accept the mystery of how the divine and human could be united in Jesus that has caused them to propose alternative theories that make up the catalog of heretical teachings.

John's affirmation that Jesus knew that he had come from God and was returning to God brings into focus what I meant when I stated that Jesus was conscious of his deity while still being human. The mystery of Luke 2:52 mentioned in the first chapter is a worthy starting point: "Jesus grew in wisdom and stature, and in favor with God and men." We are immediately confronted with the questions, What did he know, and when did he know it? His growth physically from infancy to maturity is not hard for us to imagine because we watch children along the same trajectory. But how did Jesus grow in terms of his knowledge, his psyche, and especially his self-awareness? At age twelve he was in the temple engaged in debate with the teachers of the law, but we have no reason to believe that he necessarily had been born with encyclopedic knowledge of the Bible or physics or chemistry or mathematics. But at the close of that account, when his parents found him there, he asked them, "Didn't you know I had to be in my Father's house?"—expressing a highly advanced sense of self-awareness.

As you read the Gospels, have you wondered as I have if there were not times when Jesus might have had or been tempted by some rather human thoughts? Luke tells us that some months into Jesus' ministry, "Jesus' mother and brothers came to see him, but they were not able to get near him because of the crowd. Someone told him, 'Your mother and brothers are standing outside, wanting to see you.'" Some biblical commentators have suggested that the reason Jesus' mother and brothers came to see him was that they wanted to take him home with them to Nazareth. Jesus' brothers, we are told, did not believe in his divine nature at this juncture, and the commentators speculate that they thought his ministry was getting out of control and proving to be an embarrassment. They might well have believed he had lost touch with reality (see Mark 3:21). When his own family doubted and questioned him, it would have been easy for Jesus to be tempted with his own doubts.

Similar doubts were expressed to Jesus by John the Baptist—his cousin, forerunner, and the prophet who baptized Jesus in the Jordan at the beginning of his ministry. John was later arrested by Herod and put in prison for some time. John would die in Herod's custody at the request of Herodias (see Matthew 14), but before he died he sent messengers to Jesus: "Are you the one who was to come, or should we expect someone else?" (Luke 7:20). That John, languishing in prison, was having significant doubts about who Jesus was is significant. Jesus sent back a strong and positive response: "Go back and report to John what you have seen and heard: The blind receive sight, the lame walk, those who have leprosy are cured, the deaf hear, the dead are raised, and the good news is preached to the poor" (v. 22). Yet again, Jesus might have been tempted in his human psyche to doubt his own identity because the challenge to his self-awareness came from one so close and with whom Jesus had such history.

I do not want to make too much out of the possible doubts that Jesus might have faced except to underscore how Jesus' life was marked by a growing self-awareness of his unique identity that might have been vulnerable at times because of his humanity. A final piece of evidence comes from the baptism and temptation of Jesus in the wilderness that we considered in the previous chapter. Immediately preceding his forty days in the wilderness, Jesus was baptized by John. As Jesus exited the water, a voice came from heaven: "You are my Son, whom I love; with you I am well pleased" (Luke 3:22).

It is not a stretch—in my opinion—to connect this affirmation of his identity with the testing and temptation from the hand of Satan that immediately followed: "If you are the Son of God . . ."

It appears that Satan was trying to get into Jesus' head—to sow sufficient doubt in his divine-human psyche that he would then bite on the temptation in order to "prove" he was who he knew himself to be. The voice from heaven came at a critical time in Jesus' life to strengthen his self-awareness of his identity before Satan's testing— Are you really sure you are the Son of God? Three times Satan voices the challenge to Jesus that would later come from his mother and brothers, from John the Baptist, and from his critics and adversaries. With the loving and familiar voice from heaven still in his heart and mind, Jesus could put away any doubts that Satan or anyone else would dangle before him.

Admittedly, we have had to travel a long way to get to this, but it may serve to buttress the importance of John's statement that Jesus "knew he had come from God and was returning to God." It is no casual comment or throwaway line. It represents, instead, the culmination of a growing and maturing self-awareness unique to the psyche of the Son of God. We may not be able to answer precisely the question of what Jesus knew and when he knew it, but as the evening meal began on Thursday, marking the start of Jesus' passion, he had no lingering doubts about who he was. He came from God. He would be returning to God. All of Jesus' psychological and spiritual health and strength flow from this self-awareness. And because he was fully human and would suffer in the flesh as well as in the spirit, he needed what this kedge would afford him.

WHAT JESUS' SENSE OF IDENTITY MEANS

For a Christ follower, the ultimate source of our identity comes from love that falls from a tree, the cross. Like the lyrics from The Who, we have experienced brokenness on our knees. There we have acknowledged that our mouths are at times like sewers. And, we have been kissed by the Son. We stand in awe and wonder at how God can love us. At the heart of our faith is a transforming encounter with the love of God in Christ. John summarized our faith when he wrote: "We know that we live in him and he in us, because he has given us of his Spirit. And we have seen and testify that the Father has sent his Son to be the Savior of the world. If anyone acknowledges that Jesus is the Son of God, God lives in him and he in God. And so we know and rely on the love God has for us" (1 John 4:13–16).

Because we know we do not measure up, because our mouths still spew out sewage from time to time, and because we fail often and must repeatedly return to the cross from which love flows, we each struggle at times with the assurance of our salvation and consequently the assurance of our identity as a child of God. John wrote his first epistle to address the issue of assurance: "I write these things to you who believe in the name of the Son of God so that you may know that you have eternal life" (1 John 5:13). Does it come to us as a new thought that there is a close connection between the sense of assurance of our salvation and our sense of identity? I think not for most of us.

Our identity is rooted in our relationship to Christ; and if that relationship is filled with doubt, then our sense of identity will be compromised to the same degree. Acknowledging that there is always some wobble between our profession of faith and how we live, we are cognizant that there will always be some gap where doubts can germinate into the fruit of uncertainty of our identity. The goal must be to eliminate any doubts about our relationship to Christ to the end that we will grow into an increasingly healthy sense of our identity. The very good news is that for those of us who seek to grow in our Christ-centered identity, a rich supply of Scripture will nourish us as well as encourage us: "How great is the love the Father has lavished on us, that we should be called children of God! And that is who we are! . . . Dear friends, now we are children of God, and what we will be has not yet been made known. But we know that when he appears, we shall be like him, for we shall see him as he is. Everyone who has this hope in him purifies himself, just as he is pure" (1 John 3:1–3).

That is who I am, and who you are if you belong to Jesus Christ by faith. Of course, we don't always live in the full realization of that reality on the journey we call the Christian life. Our sins and doubts undermine our sense of identity as children of God. John in his letter to his friends wrote: "Dear friends, if our hearts do not condemn us, we have confidence before God and receive from him anything we ask, because we obey his commands and do what pleases him" (1 John 3:21–22).

Our problem at times is that our hearts do condemn us. Mine does. We are still immature. We have unresolved sin in our lives and we conclude, especially when prompted by the evil one, that because of that sin God has abandoned us.

Recently I was in a large electronics chain store you would know. I had made what I thought was a good buy of a video game for my son. When we opened the game at home, we discovered it was a pirated copy that did not work on his Xbox. A closer look at the poorly printed disk label confirmed our suspicion. I took the game and the packaging back to the store for an exchange. The manager told me he could not make an exchange because, he said, "You did not buy that game disk at this store." But I did, just the day before. What he was implying was that I bought a good copy at the store and then took it home and swapped it with a pirated copy. He was calling me a thief. In a split second, I lost it. I argued angrily, I raised my voice, and I threatened never to do business with his chain of stores again (we both knew I had been a very good customer). He refused to budge, believing it was impossible for a pirated copy to have been in his inventory. I seethed with anger and stormed out, knowing that the disk had indeed come from that store.

As I started the car, all rationalizations had kicked in: *I am right! I did buy the disk here! There was no swap! I am not a thief!* Internal recriminations followed those thoughts almost immediately: *Wow! Is that how a follower of Jesus behaves? Didn't Jesus say, "You have heard that it was said to the people long ago, 'Do not murder, and anyone who murders will be subject to judgment.' But I tell you that anyone who is angry with his brother will be subject to judgment"?*

A dozen other verses burst into my increasingly guilty consciousness, including those that challenged me to examine my assurance of salvation. I was reminded again that nearly forty years since giving my life to Christ, I had not experienced a purified heart—my heart was no different from a murderer's. The result was not just guilt but a disturbing sense of uneasiness about the reality of my status as a child of God. I've been a Christian for four decades and have successfully wrapped around myself the various cloaks of reverend and pastor and doctor and professor. But in a few moments of unprotected vulnerability, my sinful nature—still alive and well, deep beneath all the cloaks—erupted violently "like a sewer hole," and I was scared. Which is my real identity? The one I have crafted or layered around myself or the one that burst to the surface in the store?

Even Dietrich Bonhoeffer, who died for his unrelenting commitment to the truth of God's Word, struggled with his own identity in light of his own inconsistencies. In a poem written after months in prison and just a month before his execution in May 1945, he expressed these struggles:

> Who am I? They often tell me I stepped from my cell's confinement calmly, cheerfully, firmly, like a squire from his country-house.
>
> Who am I? They often tell me I used to speak to my warders freely and friendly and clearly, as though it were mine to command.
>
> Who am I? They also tell me I bore the days of misfortune equally, smilingly, proudly, like one accustomed to win.

Am I then really all that which other men tell of?
Or am I only what I know of myself? Restless and
longing and sick, like a bird in a cage, struggling for
breath, as though hands were compressing my throat,
yearning for colors, for flowers, for the voices of birds,
thirsting for words of kindness, for neighborliness,
trembling with anger at despotisms and petty humiliation, tossing in expectation of great events, powerlessly
trembling for friends at an infinite distance, weary and
empty at praying, at thinking, at making, faint, and
ready to say farewell to it all?

Who am I? This or the other? Am I one person
today, and tomorrow another? Am I both at once? A
hypocrite before others, and before myself a contempt-
ibly woebegone weakling? Or is something within me
still like a beaten army, fleeing in disorder from victory
already achieved?

Who am I? They mock me, these lonely questions
of mine.

Whoever I am, Thou knowest, O God, I am
thine.[6]

Although Catholic Thomas Merton is not as widely known or
appreciated among most Protestants as the Lutheran Bonhoeffer, I
find that he has my number also. He described me well in *Seeds of
Contemplation*:

To work out our own identity in God, which the Bible
calls "working out our salvation," is a labor that requires sacrifice and anguish, risk and many tears. . . .
The secret of my identity is hidden in Him.

. . . Every one of us is shadowed by an illusory person, a false self. To say I was born in sin is to say I
came into the world with a false self. . . . All sin starts

from the assumption that my false self, the self that exists only in my own egocentric desires is the fundamental reality of life to which everything else in the universe is ordered. Thus I use up my life in the desire for pleasure and the thirst for experiences, for power, honor, knowledge and love, to clothe this false self and construct its nothingness into something objectively real. And I wind experiences around myself with pleasures and glory like bandages in order to make myself perceptible to myself and to the world, as if I were an invisible body that could only become visible when something visible covered its surface.

. . . But there is no substance under the things with which I am clothed. I am hollow. And my structure of pleasures and ambitions has no foundation.

. . . The secret to my identity is hidden in the love and mercy of God.[7]

One thing is certain: I will never resolve my identity by wrapping myself in pleasures or power or titles or accomplishments. In fact, if I am going to resolve my struggle with identity, I must allow God to cut away all the layers that enshroud me, to enable me to see me as he sees me, and then to believe that, now that we both see me, he still loves me. It is not unlike the process C. S. Lewis described in *The Chronicles of Narnia*. One of the sons of Adam is transformed into a dragon. The dragon skin must be removed; a painful process is this molting, but it is the only way. In the end his real being is revealed both to himself and to Aslan.

Of course, I might easily have rationalized my behavior—I was overreacting to my outburst in the store. There is, I rationalize, sin in all of our lives; none of us is yet perfected. But as Dallas Willard so clearly articulated in *The Divine Conspiracy*, God is working in our lives to transform our inner being, not to simply make us more effective "sin managers" (people who know how to sin less than others or even less than they used to).[8] So God wants to change me at the core level of my being, not so I will become a person who sins less but a person whose heart and resulting attitudes and actions are transformed because I am a new person in Christ, to make me into a person whose response is not to sin, whose response to adverse situations does not emanate from my old sinful nature but from my new nature in Christ. That is God's purpose in my life. When something erupted out of my heart that day, I had to ask hard questions, not about my "sin management" skills but about the nature of my heart. I had to ask about the nature of my identity: "Who are you? Who? Who? Who? Who?" God will have to rip away a few things to get to that level in my life, and I suspect in yours as well. God wants to produce that kind of maturity in me. The issues of my identity (I am a child of God) and God's sovereign control in my life (no temptation comes to me greater than I can bear) are central to that process.

MEASURING OUR GRIP ON OUR IDENTITY

Among the things that have helped me with the process of learning my identity in Christ are some lessons encountered early in my spiritual journey. Although I remember these concepts clearly, I am less certain who taught them to me.[9] Maturity, I was instructed, is a three-phased process that involves self-orientation, self-control, and self-extension.

Self-orientation refers to an increasingly strong sense of who you are: strengths, weaknesses, good habits and bad, gifts, biases, fears, dreams, insecurities, and so on. We learn about ourselves in relationship. Swiss physician and psychologist Paul Tournier wrote insightfully that it is impossible to get to know ourselves apart from a significant relationship with another person.[10] So in our close relationships with family, with the family of God, and with God himself, we learn about ourselves. Of course, nothing holds a mirror before us like marriage. In marriage so much of the real person is revealed that sometimes marriages don't survive, especially if the foundation was inadequate or the skills were not developed for processing this mutual (and sometimes frightening) revelation. But this growing self-orientation is an important part of getting to know who we are, of learning our identity.

Self-control is the second aspect of maturity. Self-control is not just better sin management. Self-control is a work of the Holy Spirit to help us close the gap between who we are and what God desires us to become. Self-control is not primarily a negation—what we don't do. It is equally a positive expression—discipline means that we do the things that will cause us to grow. Paul was thinking about positive self-control when he told Timothy that "physical training is of some value, but [training for] godliness has value for all things, holding promise for both the present life and the life to come" (1 Timothy 4:8).

To become mature we must apply three techniques of self-control: deny, delay, and detour. Whether what we have to deal with is good or bad, right or wrong, we still need to apply these principles. Not only are there bad things that we must deny, but some things that are good must be denied because they keep us from what is better or best. Jesus would not have sinned if he had turned stones into bread, but he denied the challenge of Satan because it would have kept him from what was better. Again, we must delay certain things in our lives. We must delay some good things because the timing is wrong. Occasionally, we must delay some things because we will not know until later if they are good or bad—after we have a more mature perspective. Obviously, some things in life we simply must steer clear of because we recognize our vulnerability to certain temptations.

The very sexually charged environment in which we find ourselves in the twenty-first century reveals a desperate need—especially for those who claim to be followers of Jesus—for using this trio of disciplined responses to sexuality. George Barna's studies have regularly demonstrated that Christians are often indistinguishable from their non-Christian friends with regard to sexual behavior. According to *Christianity Today*, there is little denying, little delaying (as in delaying until marriage), and very little detouring being applied among many Christians in the United States eighteen to thirty-five years.[11] That is especially true regarding the pornography that nearly overwhelms the Internet. We might pray, "Deliver us from evil" but knowingly allow ourselves to be put into compromised situations. The culture is oversaturated with compromising influences, from coed dorms (what were they thinking?) to MTV and hundreds of additional channels of television.

There appear to be two primary reasons that learning self-control in the sphere of sexuality is critical to our spiritual identity and ultimate spiritual maturity. First, our sexuality reaches to the core of our being unlike anything else. We are sexual beings. If we are ever to be more than just sexual beings controlled by sexual desires or instincts, we must first gain some self-control by denying, delaying, and detouring gratification appropriately. If we are to come to a full understanding of what it means to be children of God, we must deal with our sexuality and put it in its proper place in our lives.

Paul was careful to point out that sexual sin is unlike any other because it is a sin we commit against our own bodies (1 Corinthians 6:18). Sexual sin damages us. Second, nothing impairs our ability to hear and discern the voice of God like sexual sin. In my years of counseling men and women who were trapped in sexual sin, there was a consistent reality—people involved in sexual sin usually cease to hear God's voice or sense his presence. Because of the depth and determining nature of our sexuality, a Christian who is entangled in sexual sin is almost certain to have a struggle with his or her identity as a child of God. We will take up other impairments to our identity as a child of God in the next chapter, but certainly this one is among the most common.

Have we grasped the importance of delayed gratification for our spiritual health and progress on our spiritual path? I am not sure I have successfully taught it to my children, so it is unsettling that M. Scott Peck wrote that delayed gratification is "the only decent way to live . . . [but adolescents] are resentful of any attempt to intervene in their lifestyle of impulsiveness." He went on to add that the feeling of being loved and valued as a person is "the cornerstone of self-discipline," including delayed gratification. When we consider ourselves valuable and loved, we are willing to nurture and take care of ourselves in all the necessary ways.[12] Knowing we are "God's chosen people, holy and dearly loved" by God is essential to self-discipline. Self-discipline, in turn, is essential for a mature understanding of our identity, and a firm grasp on our identity is a most essential anchor for our lives during times of trouble.

Self-extension, the third aspect of the maturity triad, is the process by which my sphere of influence continues to expand as I continue to mature. Self-extension, of course, can be very selfish. Some seek vast networks of contacts and promote themselves in order to influence people for their own gain. The self-extension of mature faith is an increasing sphere of influence for the purpose of ministering and serving others. Some have been enabled by God to reach vast numbers of people for the sake of the kingdom. When a pastor in Kenya who has no education and no library can ride his bicycle on Saturday to a neighboring village, download Rick Warren's sermon at an Internet cafe, and then preach it to his congregation on Sunday, we see a demonstration of how a person can extend the impact of his life, virtually without boundaries.

Doug Nichols is one of my heroes because his life is all about self-extension. A missionary leader who has endured much for the kingdom, he has seen his life extended around the world. Among the many compelling stories recorded about Doug's missionary journey are the stories of his confinement in a tuberculosis sanatorium in India as a green rookie and the account of Doug's trip to Rwanda much later in life while battling cancer. He went to care for orphaned children, knowing he might likely die on the trip. (See Appendix 1.)

In order for us to move to mature self-extension, we must have a kingdom perspective and a kingdom mind-set based on a clear sense of our identity and God's ability to accomplish his will on earth as it is in heaven: "You are a chosen people, a royal priesthood, a holy nation, a people belonging to God, *that you may declare the praises of him who called you out of darkness into his wonderful light*" (1 Peter 2:9, emphasis added). Our identity as children of God brings the mandate inherent in self-extension. While not all of us have the opportunity to extend the influence of our lives to the whole world like Rick Warren or Doug Nichols, we will never attain maturity without understanding that we are children of God and that we are about the work of the family business, to expand the kingdom of God the Father. Because he was growing increasingly aware of his identity and its implications, Jesus told Mary and Joseph that he had to be about his Father's business. We will come to the same conclusion when we mature and arrive at a full understanding of who we are.

FINDING OUR IDENTITY IN CHRIST

Our struggle with a personal sense of identity is usually in proportion to our lack of maturity. A lack of maturity is not only a result of not being old enough but also of not being proactive enough. Some people propose that we do not come to a settled view of the world and our place in it (our identity) until we are in our early twenties. Rather than continuing to refine our maps, which requires effort, we believe that our maps are complete and correct and spend the rest of our lives defending them. When we do this, we run the risk of stunted self-orientation, self-absorption rather than self-extension, and indulgence or impulsiveness instead of self-control as we seek instead to wrap around ourselves various experiences, possessions, and pleasures.

Being a twin greatly magnified the identity crisis I suffered as an adolescent. Entering a high school freshman class of 1,350 students (the school had nearly 3,500 students) certainly made my search for identity more difficult. Out of this sea of images and impressions that I recall years later, one voice emerged. It was the voice of God— spoken not from heaven but from the lips of a man named Doug, the new Young Life staff guy in our suburban Chicago region. Doug spoke with God's voice, and I heard it. The first message came in one word: "Bob." Here was a man who not only loved high school kids in general, he loved me enough to know me and call me by name. Being called by my own name in the crowd at a football game or in the halls at school—after sixteen years of "BobbyDickie" and "Which one are you?"—was a powerful thing. Doug and I became close friends, as close as a sixteen-year-old and twenty-six-year-old can be. He later recalled that I was the most cynical teenager he ever encountered. Doug and I continue to be friends more than forty years later; and he continued until age seventy to work with kids. His love shattered the cynicism that was part of my false self. How thankful I am that he loved me and eventually loved me into the kingdom of God. At the A&W Root Beer Drive-In, overlooking a driving range one day after school, I asked Doug how I could know if I was a child of God. He answered me from God's Word, and my heart began to change. As I look back on that interaction, what I wanted to know centered on my identity: how could I know I was a child of God? To know that would be to know who I am. Forty years later to know that is still to know who I am.

I'll not belabor the story of my journey. Many stories are far more significant than mine. But my first step toward a fully developed sense of identity was monumental. I still had major steps to take. I struggled with going to seminary and into the ministry because of a lingering negative identity. After I was past thirty, I began to work through the Pastor Bob identity. Maturity does not happen quickly.

Whenever we struggle with our sense of identity, we need to strengthen our understanding that we are nothing less than adopted children of God. Although we are still works in progress, we need assurance that we belong to Jesus Christ. In reality we do not hold on to him; it is he who holds on to us. Knowing who we are is our first anchor in times of difficulty. We need to make sure the rope that holds the first anchor is adequate, strong, and inspected regularly. This anchor also will surely be tested; Satan will ask us, "If you really are a child of God, what are you doing in this situation?". When that happens, our sense of identity will be our anchor. In the next chapter we will explore more fully the important matter of identity as we discover how God's method for grasping our identity is 180 degrees opposite from the principles the world offers.

4

ANCHOR 1:
LEARNING WHO WE ARE (PART 2)

IF A MAN REMAINS IN ME AND I IN HIM, HE WILL
BEAR MUCH FRUIT; APART FROM ME YOU CAN DO
NOTHING.

It was hanging on the wall of the pressroom of my father's printing company. The senior press operator who owned it would not take it down. He couldn't understand why other employees were bothered by it. His refusal to take it down continued, and tension mounted. Words were spoken. Then unkind words were spoken. Finally someone took it and hid it where it could not be found.

The offensive item was a wall clock, ordinary in most ways, except that the hands ran backward and the numbers were placed on the clock accordingly. The clock never bothered me, but it bothered others. It was not that time ran in reverse, just the clock. It ran backward and caused enormous anxiety in people who were unable, for whatever reason, to adjust to a clock that ran counterclockwise.

The Common System for Establishing Our Identity

We have considered previously the matter of our identity and how we can discover that identity as followers of Jesus. I want go further in this chapter to compare and contrast how many people—including no small number of Christians—seek to gain their identity according to the principles of the world. The common process by which many seek to gain or establish their identity runs counter-clockwise—opposite from God's design. God's design for our identity is so counterintuitive to our secular culture that most people—including Christians—don't even see that the clock is running in reverse. In John 15 we find a model for identity and health, a process that Jesus modeled and clearly laid out for us.

It seems almost too obvious. For most in the North American culture, our identity is derived from our material possessions, what we accomplish, what titles we hold, and what assets—such as beauty or relationships—we have. A quick scan through nearly any magazine today will validate this observation.

In a world of haves and have-nots, the competition for status is a competition for identity. We are bombarded by entertainment

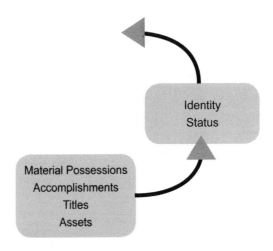

award shows where possessions and assets are flaunted for "stars" in competition for status and an identity to distinguish them among the dazzling crowd. Each year multimillion-dollar athletes seek to renegotiate their contracts because in the year or two since they signed, other athletes in their sport have become the highest paid, and they cannot tolerate being "dissed" this way. It's not the money, mind you; it's the recognition. It is the identity as the highest paid in a sport, or in an era, or at a position that they seek. Of course, when status and identity become a competitive pursuit, the higher a person seeks to climb, increasingly fewer spots exist on the pyramid.

The problem with an identity based on accomplishments, possessions, and assets is its very fleeting nature. Former TV actors (who like to be called "stars") and former athletes alike reveal how transitory this identity can be, as well as how demanding a master it becomes. As elderly celebrities die, it is not uncommon for them to be identified or eulogized in terms of a major role they played decades before. When Bob Denver died in 2005, the news media told us that Gilligan had died; and everyone knew immediately to whom they were referring. Poor Bob Denver! His identity for forty years had been linked to a role he assumed for ninety-eight half-hour episodes during three seasons of a TV sitcom in the mid-1960s. From age thirty until his death at seventy, his identity revolved around the character of Gilligan. (Then again, there is Kato Kaelin, whose identity is still wrapped up in having rented a room from O. J. Simpson.) I don't want to suggest that Bob Denver was not a good and kind person or that he had no life after 1966. I'm uncertain about all that. Nevertheless, he serves as a poster child for those who are stuck with or who seek an identity based on accomplishments or possessions.

Of course, former stars are not the only ones who struggle with issues of identity. We all do in a culture where one question we ask when meeting someone for the first time is, "And what do you do?" We quickly and easily evaluate people based on what they do. There is a well-known but unwritten hierarchy of professions that serves as a grid by which North Americans tend to evaluate the relative worth of people. (I find that people treat me one way when they see "Dr." attached to my name and assume I am a physician. They treat me differently when they discover instead that "Dr." refers to my doctor of ministry degree.) Moreover, because so many people use this grid, we consciously or unconsciously seek our own affirmation and identity based on what we do. So being retired is a status symbol that increases as the retirement age decreases, while being unemployed is an embarrassment—even though there might not be much difference between the two on a daily basis.

Christians are not immune. In countless churches and parachurch ministries, if the truth were told, qualification for leadership is often based on a person's job status, ability to give money, and success in a profession. Plumbers and taxi drivers—however spiritual they may be—are disproportionately underrepresented on elder boards of evangelical churches. The boards of Christian ministries, agencies, and colleges list their members by name and the most prestigious title or description available. The widespread influence of our culture has resulted in a trend to base leadership in the church on what is valued in the business community more often than on the biblical model, which is the family. Paul wrote that to lead in the church a man must demonstrate his ability to lead not in the *agora*, the marketplace, but in the home (1 Timothy 3:2–5)!

In our distinct evangelical subculture, our own grid has mesmerized us. For pastors, the size of their churches matter greatly. Megachurch pastors have a higher status and a more desirable identity (status) than a journeyman pastor of a smaller church. For many, the TV rating and number of stations airing the ministry become the measures of worth. Church planters and bivocational pastors in the inner city are well down on the chart, just above missionaries. With the dramatic growth of satellite television, the Internet, and the Christian recording industry, an evangelical celebrity class has emerged. Having rubbed shoulders with the evangelical celebrity class over the past few years, I find at times that "Holy-wood" is not much different than Hollywood. Although we give appropriate verbal affirmation that this is God's work and not ours, the totem pole still stands.

The apostle John, the source of so many of our examined biblical truths, gave a warning for those who would seek identity based on possessions or accomplishments: "For everything in the world—the cravings of sinful man, the lust of his eyes and the *boasting of what he has and does*—comes not from the Father but from the world. The world and its desires pass away, but the man who does the will of God lives forever" (1 John 2:16–17, emphasis added).

The "boasting of what he has and does" is an apt description of the pursuit of the possession-and-accomplishment-based identity. While John did not tell us why this pursuit is so common and so appealing, it is not hard to comprehend. William Glasser, a secular psychologist of a generation ago, suggested in *Reality Therapy* that the most basic human needs in life are to love and be loved and to feel worthwhile to ourselves and to a significant other person. Glasser went on to make a dramatic speculation that all mental illness was the result of seeking these two basic needs in irresponsible ways.[1] Although he was not a man of faith who calculated the love of God in Christ into his formula, some truth is apparent in his paradigm for well-being. Glasser has helped me understand that the pursuit of identity and status is driven often by the desire to be loved and affirmed, and that possessions and accomplishments are means to this other end.

Let's return to the clock that runs backward.

We see the clock moving from accomplishments and possessions to identity and status and from there to love and acceptance. The problem with this clock or process, however, is that accomplishments

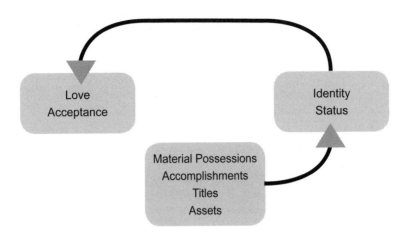

and possessions rarely lead to the corresponding love and acceptance we desire. The sad tales of lottery winners are examples. I recall a recent TV program featuring megalottery winners (the $100 million-plus kind), revealed how dysfunctional this process is. One pathetic lottery winner acknowledged that he earns $22,000 daily on his fortune and "needs to spend" that much each day on things to put in his home—suits of armor, engraved elephant tusks, a collection of muscle cars—where he lives alone. He acknowledged that he didn't have a telephone any longer because he was tired of friends and relatives who wanted something from him. Indeed, many of those who have accomplished or attained much are chronicled as least successful in finding love and acceptance. It is little wonder that this clock that runs backward is as frustrating as it is. To paraphrase Paul, now let me show you a better way.

THE BIBLICAL MODEL FOR IDENTITY

God created us as relational beings, and our need for love is unapologetically part of how God made us. Our Creator also provided for that basic need to be met on both the horizontal and vertical axes of life. He loves his creation, having created us to live in a loving relationship with him. He also created us with the capacity for meaningful love relationships with one another—husbands and wives, family members, and dear friends. I believe Glasser was correct when he said that our major problems are caused by our efforts to meet our basic needs in irresponsible ways, whether by promiscuity as a substitute for real love, outlandish attention-getting behavior, or addictions. He correctly posited that "without the key person through whom we gain strength and encouragement to cope with reality," we lapse into seeking our foundational needs in unrealistic ways.[2]

What Glasser did not grasp is that because of the corruption of sin and results of the fall, we are predisposed to seeking to meet our basic needs in irresponsible ways, in counterproductive ways, even in self-destructive ways. Because of our sin, we find it difficult to give and receive love. We often find intimacy difficult and therefore seek love in alternate ways. We also seek to meet our basic needs in ways that often disregard or trample over others in pursuit of these most basic needs.

God has a new paradigm that leads us to health and meets our two most basic needs in life. The good news of the gospel is that we do not need to settle for a clock that runs backward and is destined to frustrate us. Jesus described this model for health very simply in John 15. Jesus and his disciples had finished their last meal together and then went out from the city to the Mount of Olives. As they passed the south facade of the temple in Jerusalem, they saw the huge gold vine that adorned that main entrance into the temple precincts. The vine had long been the symbol for Israel. Even to this day, the likeness of Joshua and Caleb carrying huge clusters of grapes out from the Promised Land is the logo of the Israeli tourism board. Israel was God's vineyard. As the disciples passed the temple, Jesus set the record straight about the vine: "I am the true vine, and my Father is the gardener. He cuts off every branch in me that bears no fruit, while every branch that does bear fruit he prunes so that it will be even more fruitful" (John 15:1–2).

Israel was not a fruitful vine for God. It had not been for perhaps hundreds of years. As Jesus had earlier told the Pharisees, Israel would soon be cut off and a new branch of God's servants would bear fruit for him. This new expression of the kingdom of God on earth, to be called the church, would be established and empowered to bear the life and fruit of the true vine, Jesus himself.

Jesus then turned his attention to those who would be part of this new movement of God: "You are already clean because of the word I have spoken to you. Remain in me, and I will remain in you. No branch can bear fruit by itself; it must remain in the vine. Neither can you bear fruit unless you remain in me. I am the vine; you are the branches. If a man remains in me and I in him, he will bear much fruit; apart from me you can do nothing" (vv. 3–5).

In these few sentences Jesus provided for his church, his new covenant people, a new paradigm for health that is 180 degrees from the paradigm of the world. Jesus began with acceptance. He did not end there; he began there: "You are already clean because of the word I have spoken to you." Our great need for love and acceptance does not come at the end of a cycle that begins with accomplishments and possessions in search of identity. For those who have come and received the grace of God, acceptance is the starting place! We are clean! We have been pruned! The word picture in the original language involves a play on words between lifting and cleaning. God, by his word, has lifted us up and carefully cleaned us as a vinedresser does with growing clusters of grapes. The Bible refers to this saving work in many ways, including the washing of regeneration, justification, and sanctification. Here God declares that we are clean. It happens when we come to faith in Christ and receive the word of God. That is why Jesus says we are clean "because of the word" spoken to us. It is because we have received the word of God by faith that God has accepted us.

Acceptance from God based on receiving the word and the work of Jesus is our starting point. The acceptance—the foundation for what Glasser called "feeling worthwhile to ourselves and another significant individual"—is already ours. While we know we are inherently sinful, we can still feel worthwhile because God has demonstrated our worth. While we were still his enemies, Christ died for us, the result of which is that there is no condemnation for those who are in him (Romans 8:1). We have been loved fully by the most significant one, our Father in heaven. As a result, we have the remarkable status as children of God: "Dear friends, now we are children of God, and what we will be has not yet been made known" (1 John 3:2).

As we return to our model, we recognize that it moves in a clockwise direction, beginning at nine o'clock.

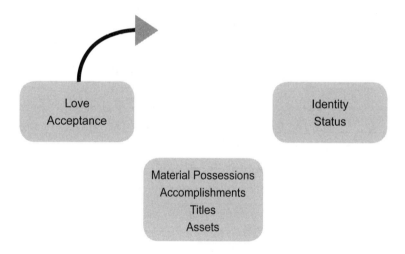

Quite the opposite of the world's model for health, Jesus next declared a different pattern where the love and acceptance of the Father through the Word of God is the beginning point—the source of our identity: "I am the vine; you are the branches." In that single compound sentence is the essence of our identity. He is the vine; we who belong to him by faith are branches. Our identity is relationally determined—not determined by what we do or what we accomplish. Jesus' statement invites us to no longer seek our identity in what we do or have, but to increasingly find our identity in our relationship to Christ. It does not happen at once—it is a process whereby our identity in Christ emerges, grows, and solidifies as we allow God's Spirit to transform us (our identity) by the renewing of our minds (Romans 12:1–2).

In God's design there is still a place in our lives for accomplishments and, to a certain degree, possessions. However, in the biblical model, what we accomplish is not the source of our identity but the result of our increasing sense of identity in Christ. Jesus said to the Eleven: "This is to my Father's glory, that you bear much fruit, showing yourselves to be my disciples" (John 15:8).

God's desire is that we live fruitful lives. It is not limited to fruit for the kingdom of God, but certainly that is an important part of a fruitful life. We are told that whatever our hand finds to do that we should do it as to the Lord (Colossians 3:23–24). We may not all prosper as Joseph did in Egypt when he sought to be fruitful for God, even in prison. We should and can be fruitful writers, students, entrepreneurs, butchers, bakers, and candlestick makers. We can all pray as Moses did: "Establish the works of our hands for us—yes, establish the work of our hands" (Psalm 90:17). God is glorified and we invest in his kingdom when we are fruitful and fulfilled for the kingdom. God is glorified when his kingdom is our passion and desire. Many of us have learned much from John Piper, well-known author and pastor of Bethlehem Baptist Church in Minneapolis, who suggested a restatement of the opening of the Westminster Shorter Catechism of faith:

Q. What is the chief end of man?

A. The chief end of man is to glorify God by enjoying him forever.[3]

Nothing we do gives greater glory to God than being fruitful for his kingdom and enjoying it along the way. The psalm writer put it into one of the contemporary songs of the eighth century BC: "You have made known to me the path of life; you will fill me with joy in your presence, with eternal pleasures at your right hand." (Psalm 16:11).

Our accomplishments are not, however, the basis of our identity. They cannot be. Jesus was blunt enough: "Apart from me you can do nothing" How can we seek to make our fruitfulness for his kingdom the source of our identity or take pride and boast in what we have and do if we internalize this truth? John Piper argued further that "the most dangerous thing in the world is the sin of self-reliance." Within the illusion of self-reliance (the clock that runs counterclockwise), we are easily tempted to see prosperity or fruitfulness for the kingdom as our sources of affirmation or worth or identity. The model for health that Jesus taught the disciples now comes full circle. Almost.

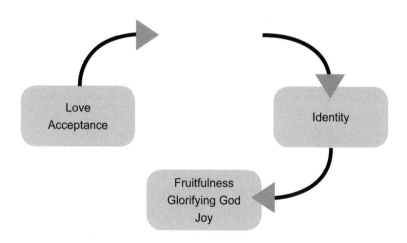

Not all of us find the Christian life fruitful, fulfilling, or joyful, of course, because what is missing from the model may be missing from our lives: "*Remain in me*, and I will remain in you. No branch can bear fruit by itself; it must *remain* in the vine. Neither can you bear fruit unless you *remain in me*. I am the vine; you are the branches. If a man *remains in me* and I in him, he will bear much fruit; apart from me you can do nothing" (John 15:4–5, emphasis added).

The point is clear enough. If we are abiding, we will have a growing understanding of our identity and our purpose in life. Remaining is an organic process. A branch draws its life from the vine and must remain connected. When a branch is broken, it is in jeopardy of losing the life-giving nutrients from the vine.

At this juncture it is important to acknowledge that volumes have been written on the subject of abiding in Christ, spiritual disciplines, and spiritual formation based on this passage. I do not want to suggest that John 15 is primarily about identity. It is not. It is about abiding—and a secure identity is a critical byproduct. Knowing who we are in Christ—deep in the heart of our being—is essential and can only be attained and preserved by abiding in Christ.

If we do not nurture our relationship, we easily forget who we are in Christ and drift away from the purpose for which God purchased us with the blood of Christ. For years as a pastor, I attempted to teach people the supremacy of glorifying God as the purpose for our lives. I was startled to realize how often this was a totally new concept for many longtime followers of Christ. The conviction that I have long held, that many Christians simply do not understand their purpose, was confirmed by the enormous sales of Rick Warren's *The Purpose Driven Life*. This best seller—demonstrating how widespread the lack of understanding was—has come like water on dry ground.

Glen Packiam, my neighbor in Colorado Springs and author of *Secondhand Jesus*, spoke pointedly of the life of Henri Nouwen, who wrote:

> After twenty five years in the academic world as a teacher of pastoral psychology, pastoral theology and

> Christian spirituality, I began to experience a deep inner threat. As I entered into my fifties . . . I came face to face with the simple question, "Did becoming older bring me closer to Jesus?"
>
> Everyone was saying that I was doing really well, but something inside me was telling me that my success was putting my own soul in danger. I began to ask myself if my lack of contemplative prayer, my loneliness, and my constantly changing involvement in what seemed most urgent were signs that the Spirit was gradually being suppressed.[4]

Seeking to bear fruit while living a spiritual life of disconnect can only lead to burnout, as it did for Nouwen. Seeking our identity from our accomplishments—even teaching at Harvard and other accomplishments that others would regard as "doing really well"—may lead to status but can never lead to a healthy identity as a dearly loved child of God. The counterclockwise system will always lead to burnout. But for the Christian who begins at the right starting point and moves clockwise, the same outcome is likely without abiding in Christ.

If we are abiding, we will be fruitful. We will understand who we are, and we will understand our purpose: We are branches grafted into the vine in order to bear the fruit of the vine. If we are not abiding, we will find ourselves unproductive—and unfulfilled. Reflecting on a whole litany of spiritual disciplines, Peter wrote: "For if you possess these qualities in increasing measure, they will keep you from being ineffective and unproductive in your knowledge of our Lord Jesus Christ." Peter went on to say that if someone is not abiding "he is nearsighted and blind, and has forgotten [why] he has been cleansed from his past sins" (2 Peter 1:8–9).

How nearsighted we can become! I recall the life and work of astronomer Percival Lowell. While known and honored for the discovery of Planet X (which would later lead to others discovering Pluto), his greatest efforts were given to the study of Mars. For fifteen years around the turn of the twentieth century, Lowell studied Mars through a telescope in the clear air of Flagstaff, Arizona. He wrote three books on Mars, in which he collected his numerous drawings of the red planet. The drawings showed intricate networks of canals on Mars, leading many in the early part of the twentieth century to conclude that there must be some form of life there. He also made detailed drawings of the cloud-enshrouded Venus. Sadly, years later it was determined that the canals Lowell, who suffered from severe myopia, had seen in the eyepiece of his telescope were in reality reflections of his eye's blood vessels superimposed over the images of Mars.[5] Spiritual nearsightedness causes us to lose focus, lose perspective, and drift away spiritually, thinking we are focused on the right thing.

When properly oiled by faith and running as designed, Jesus' model is a marvelous engine that leads us to spiritual and emotional health. Because of our sin and the influence of all the different expressions of worldliness, Jesus' model is clearly counterintuitive and requires that by faith we abandon and renounce our pursuit of

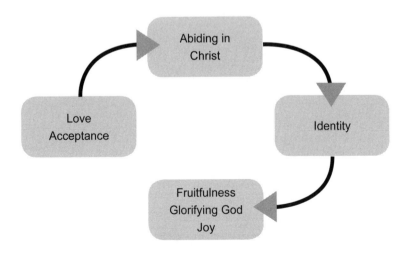

acceptance and identity rooted in accomplishment and possessions. Paul warned the church at Colossae, "See to it that no one takes you captive through hollow and deceptive philosophy, which depends on human tradition and the basic principles of this world rather than on Christ" (2:8). We are always in danger of becoming captive to the world's principles.

As Jesus came to the end of this teaching on the way to the Mount of Olives, he concluded: "I have told you this so that my joy may be in you and that your joy may be complete" (John 15:11). He had a number of distinct lessons he wanted to communicate to them on this extremely tense and emotional evening. This one is his formula, his model, for a healthy identity and the acceptance in God that we all crave. It was his joy he wanted them to have, for only his joy would enable them to experience the complete joy he intended for them. Being able to experience joy that is based on our relationship to God and serving him is essential to our spiritual, emotional, and psychological health. Jesus endured the cross because of the "joy set before him."

5

ANCHOR 2:
LEARNING WHO IS IN
CONTROL OF OUR LIVES

JESUS KNEW THAT THE FATHER HAD PUT ALL THINGS
UNDER HIS POWER, AND THAT HE HAD COME FROM
GOD AND WAS RETURNING TO GOD.

There was a second statement by John that seized me that day in 1998. John noted that as the evening meal was being served, Jesus was not only fully aware of who he was but also uniquely aware of his circumstances. He was at that moment both facing the dark storm clouds from hell gathering on the horizon and also completely in control of the moment. In an earlier chapter, we explored one aspect of Jesus' awareness of the circumstances as he spoke of the great *kairos* moment that was now on him. Here at the Last Supper John reveals the second aspect of that awareness: "Jesus knew that the Father had put all things under his power" (John 13:3).

The magnitude of this statement was not revealed in a great miraculous event that would deliver Jesus or spare him from drinking from the cup that had been prepared for him. Instead, the comprehensive nature of the statement would be revealed in a myriad of details as the pieces of the picture of his arrest, trial, scourging, and crucifixion fit together. By his authority all the prophecies of the Old Testament (many from Isaiah 53) would be fulfilled and confirm that he was the Messiah, the Holy One of Israel.

AWARE OF THE FATHER'S SOVEREIGN CONTROL

Perhaps the control issue has already become apparent as you read John's unique Gospel. As Royce Gruenler pointed out, John's Gospel reveals a fascinating juxtaposition, as Jesus had all the authority of God the Father but deferred to God the Father in all things.[1] One moment he stated that he neither did nor said anything except what the Father commanded, and just a moment later he claimed the authority of God for himself. One section from John 5 is sufficient as an example:

> Jesus gave them this answer: "I tell you the truth, the Son can do nothing by himself; he can do only what he sees his Father doing, because whatever the Father does the Son also does. For the Father loves the Son and shows him all he does. Yes, to your amazement he will show him even greater things than these. Moreover, the Father judges no one, but has entrusted all judgment to the Son, that all may honor the Son just as they honor the Father. He who does not honor the Son does not honor the Father, who sent him. . . .
>
> For as the Father has life in himself, so he has granted the Son to have life in himself. And he has given him authority to judge because he is the Son of Man. . . .
>
> By myself I can do nothing; I judge only as I hear, and my judgment is just, for I seek not to please myself but him who sent me."

While this could seem ambiguous to us, it might best be seen as a perfect balance of the Son of Man—operating fully on his own human plane while always intersecting the unseen spiritual plane where God is sovereign.

Perhaps the most curious example of this is found, appropriately, in chapter eight of John's Gospel. A woman in a jostling crowd touched Jesus' robe in hopes of finding relief from years of hemorrhaging. She was healed when she touched him. The divine and human intersected as Jesus asked who touched him but then acknowledged that healing power had gone out from him. Although the events on the night of his arrest would unfold on a human plane, Jesus was aware that on a different plane everything was under his divine control. It should come as no surprise that what unfolded that night appears catastrophic on the human plane but at the same time accomplished every detail of God's sovereign plan, placed under the operational authority of Jesus.

First, earlier that evening Jesus directed his disciples to take with them two swords as they went out from the upper room. He did so in order that the prophecy should be fulfilled that the Messiah would be arrested and therefore "numbered among criminals." Peter would use one of those small swords to cut off the ear of Malchus, the servant of the high priest. Jesus, who had all authority and was in full control of the events, not only commanded with his words that the altercation stop but also, with his touch, miraculously restored the ear of Malchus.

Second, we note that Jesus was in charge of his own arrest, something we don't see in any of the televised police reality videos. Not only did Jesus not seek to flee or evade their grasp (as he had done numerous times before when it was not his time), he stepped forward:

> Jesus, knowing all that was going to happen to him,
> went out and asked them, "Who is it you want?"
> "Jesus of Nazareth," they replied.

"I am he," Jesus said. (And Judas the traitor was standing there with them.) When Jesus said, "I am he," they drew back and fell to the ground.

Again he asked them, "Who is it you want?"

And they said, "Jesus of Nazareth."

"I told you that I am he," Jesus answered. "If you are looking for me, then let these men go." This happened so that the words he had spoken would be fulfilled: "I have not lost one of those you gave me" (John 18:4–9).

These verses remind us again that Jesus knew every detail of what would happen because it was under his authority. Remarkably, Jesus was the one who came forward and asked the question for which everyone knew the answer. In fact, he had to ask it twice. Even more remarkable was his demand (which was accepted!) that all the others should be let go. That the detachment from the temple guard should agree to this is nearly unthinkable, but again it is in fulfillment of prophecy by the authority of the one who was orchestrating all things.

But most surprising is the response of the throng that came to arrest Jesus. They fell to the ground when Jesus said, "I am he." Perhaps the best understanding is that in Aramaic Jesus spoke, "I Am," the holy and generally unspoken name of YHWH, the Lord God of Israel. Having come to arrest him, they instead bow before him, only to regain their posture and proceed to arrest him. When they fell to the ground in response to his statement of "I Am," it became clear that this was no ordinary arrest. Clearly, the Father had put all things under his authority.

Over the next eighteen hours, more prophecies were fulfilled by the authority of the one who accomplished all things according to his will: Jesus was beaten beyond recognition; he was crushed by his adversaries, yet not a bone was broken; they cast lots for his clothing in order that it not be torn apart; and after his death he was buried in a borrowed grave. These fulfilled prophecies as well as others demonstrate the Son of God's authority to orchestrate events even from the grave (that part called Paradise). The picture that emerges is clear and precise. Jesus knew that he had come from God and was returning to God; and the Father had put all things under his authority. With these two realities fully developed in his mind and heart, he was able to yield his wrists to be bound and then to be taken away as a lamb to the slaughter.

SECURE IN HIS IDENTITY

Before we move ahead too far in the narrative, we should take special note of how Jesus' refined sense of identity and authority manifested itself that evening at the Last Supper. John recorded what the Synoptic Gospels do not, that Jesus took off his outer garments, wrapped a towel around his waist, and washed the feet of the disciples—including Judas. Jesus, always humble, demonstrated his humility again with the towel and basin. He did not need the place of honor. He did not need the testimony and affirmation of men. He did not even need the friendship of those who would abandon him. He did not exercise his prerogative to summon angels to do this foot washing for him. He did not need the worship of heaven at that moment. He knew who he was and nothing at this critical juncture would diminish the self-awareness fully developed in his psyche. Because he knew, he was able to wash the disciples' feet. There was not the slightest measure of insecurity or awkwardness on Jesus' part. He did this act of service to show the extent of his love. And he left them a challenge, that those who learn from his example and who are secure in who they are ought to do as he did and wash one another's feet.

MATURE IN OUR IDENTITY

When we begin to mature in our knowledge of who we are in Christ, we find a new degree of security as we pass through difficult times. This second anchor is critical for anyone who endeavors to follow Jesus Christ. Knowing who we are serves as a kedge to take us through tribulation. The other anchor that keeps us steady is belief that since we are God's dearly loved adopted children, we can trust him in any and all circumstances. The apostle John wrote, "If anyone acknowledges that Jesus is the Son of God, God lives in him and he in God. And so we know and rely on the love God has for us" (1 John 4:15–16).

So the two statements from John that we're examining in this chapter are more clearly linked than we might first realize: Jesus knew he had come from God and was returning to God. This speaks to our knowing who we are. Jesus also knew the Father had placed all things under his authority. This speaks to our knowing who is in charge.

Dietrich Bonhoeffer wrote that every temptation we face is a temptation of Christ.[2] I believe he was correct. Often, when we encounter the really significant crises of life, we are tempted as Jesus was (allow me to paraphrase): "If you really are a child of God, what are you doing here in this particular wilderness?" We really don't have to wait for Satan to show up; it's a question we sometimes ask ourselves naturally (in the purest sense of natural). This question is part of the larger global question about the existence of evil and why God does not regularly prevent it. I've observed that this question often shows up in two hybrid forms: "If God really loves me, what am I doing in this wilderness?" and "If God is really in control, what am I doing in this situation?"

Indeed, the question of why God allowed the Holocaust or the great Asian tsunami or 9/11 represents a huge philosophical obstacle for many, blocking the path to God. This appears especially to be the case for North Americans who believe they not only have a right to pursue happiness but also an entitlement that extends to a right to happiness and a comfortable life. As one who regularly reads papers from my Introduction to Philosophy classes, I see the traces of this issue in the lives of many of my students, most of whom have a secular worldview. Although I receive from time to time the very revealing, "I could never accept a God who could send someone [read: "me"] to hell for having premarital sex," most often I read, "I cannot believe in God because of the evil and the suffering in the world."

Christians are not exempt from this North American worldview. A generation ago Francis Schaeffer's oft-repeated mantra was that twentieth-century North American Christians appeared to have only two prominent values—personal peace and affluence, their own little world to be at peace and enough money to enjoy that sphere. Unless we have the solid grasp on our faith that we can trust God to be in control when the storms of life come, we are no less inclined than non-Christians to wonder where God is and to question his goodness or his control.

Perhaps no one demonstrated the importance of this anchor in his life more than the late Dr. Jim Boice, who led the influential and historic Tenth Presbyterian Church of Philadelphia for thirty-two years as senior pastor. In 2000 he was diagnosed with liver cancer. He addressed the congregation the following Sunday morning with a powerful statement showing that he was able to find a secure anchor and knew that all things are in the Father's hands:

> Should you pray for a miracle? Well, you're free to do that, of course. My general impression is that the God who is able to do miracles is also able to keep you from getting the problem in the first place. . . .
>
> Pray for the glory of God. If you think of God glorifying himself in history . . . he did it at the cross of Jesus Christ. And it wasn't by delivering him from the cross, though he could have. . . . And yet that's where God is most glorified. . . .
>
> When things like this come into our lives, they are not accidental. It is not as if God somehow forgot what

was going on, and something bad slipped by. . . . God does everything according to his will. . . .

Everything he does is good. . . . If God does something in your life, would you change it? If you changed it, you'd make it worse. It wouldn't be as good. So that's the way we want to accept it and move forward.[3]

This is counterintuitive in our culture. When crises come, many—including those of faith—are often conditioned to somehow see their "rights" as violated and look for someone to sue or prosecute or at least someone to blame.

Our second kedge anchor, the ability to trust that God has all things under his authority, is inexorably linked to our identity as children of God called by his name. It is a place where love falls from the tree. The apostle John wrote in 1 John 3–4 that we are the children of God but that we are just beginning to comprehend what that really means. As we comprehend it, it becomes our secure anchor: "And now, dear children, continue in him, so that when he appears we may be confident and unashamed before him at his coming" (1 John 2:28). Our confidence that the one who is in total control is the lover of our souls is the result of abiding in him and grasping firmly the knowledge of who we are in him.

However, since we are just beginning to comprehend this and will not fully understand all this here on earth, we need to read, study, and meditate on passages from 1 John 3–4, but we also need to grasp Ephesians 1–3, where Paul invested the first half of his epistle documenting who we are in Christ: God "has blessed us in the heavenly realms with every spiritual blessing in Christ" (Ephesians 1:3). We might wish that we could render those passages into easy cookbook lessons, but these are passages that don't easily lend themselves to such an approach. So study and meditate we must. Then we will have an answer when Satan taunts us with the identity question, "If you really are a child of God, what are you doing here in this wilderness?" This is another of our anchors for difficult situations and times in the wilderness.

6

ANCHOR 3:
GRASPING THE TRUTH
OF GOD'S WORD

I AM THE WAY AND THE TRUTH AND THE LIFE.

Recently I have brought a new element to my classroom teaching. I now carry three small stuffed animals in my briefcase. One is a small bunny, one is a small horse, and the third is a small unicorn. I sometimes give them to students in my classes to help monitor me or the students in the class. The little beanbag animals are waved or gently tossed to me or a classmate when we are guilty of one of three infractions. The bunny is thrust into action when someone is chasing a rabbit. The horse is deployed when someone is guilty of beating a dead horse—continuing to argue long after the point has been made. And the unicorn is summoned when someone is simply not getting to the point.

All three are needed from time to time because many of us struggle with poor communication. (These stuffed animals are also suitable for committee or board meetings!) I teach preaching and coach preachers, and I admit my major classroom sin is chasing rabbits, while my major preaching sin is not coming to the point at the right time. Because the burden of communication falls on the communicator, good communicators work to find every reasonable means to communicate. In some ways we have not come very far from the ancient Greeks, who defined rhetoric as using all the available means of persuasion.

Jesus, the Word of God to humanity, had come to communicate to a reluctant and resistant audience a simple message: "The kingdom of God is near. Repent and believe the good news!" (Mark 1:15). Throughout his public ministry, Jesus used all the available means of persuasion and communication. The disciples reflected on that at the end of the Farewell Discourse: "Now you are speaking clearly and without figures of speech. Now we can see that you know all things and that you do not even need to have anyone ask you questions. This makes us believe that you came from God" (John 16:29–30).

Jesus' communication style involved didactic teaching. The Sermon on the Mount is certainly a précis of Jesus' basic teaching—perhaps given in whole or in part many times and in various settings. The Olivet Discourse in Matthew 24 is Jesus' prophetic sermon, and it also is a didactic message concerning the second advent of the Messiah. Clearly, John 14–16 is didactic in nature, as Jesus taught and exhorted (two major components of preaching) the Eleven right up to the end.

Jesus also used a form of the Socratic method that was well-known at this time, some 450 years after the brilliant but petulant Athenian. This method involved asking a series of questions, seeking with each question to push the listener to examine his beliefs and assumptions. Perhaps the classic exchange of this kind is recorded in Mark 11:27–33:

> They arrived again in Jerusalem, and while Jesus was
> walking in the temple courts, the chief priests, the

teachers of the law and the elders came to him. "By what authority are you doing these things?" they asked. "And who gave you authority to do this?"

Jesus replied, "I will ask you one question. Answer me, and I will tell you by what authority I am doing these things. John's baptism—was it from heaven, or from men? Tell me!"

They discussed it among themselves and said, "If we say, 'From heaven,' he will ask, 'Then why didn't you believe him?' But if we say, 'From men'...." (They feared the people, for everyone held that John really was a prophet.)

So they answered Jesus, "We don't know."

Jesus said, "Neither will I tell you by what authority I am doing these things."

But Jesus was also a great storyteller, leaving us with about sixty (variously counted by scholars) parables—word pictures that use an image or story to illustrate a truth (see Matthew 13). Some are as simple as the kingdom of God being like a pearl of great price. Others are very complex, such as the parable of the sower—a story Jesus used to explain to the disciples a truth concerning the Word of God. But that explanation has not necessarily made the meaning unequivocal, verifying what Jesus said—that the parables were given so that some might hear and believe and others would not. It is a curious thing that a communicator would seek to be understood by only some of his audience, yet that seems to have been Jesus' communication strategy at times.

The Son of God also communicated through actions, often involving miracles so well-known that they became part of Western cultural consciousness: he walked on water, he fed five thousand, he touched lepers, he calmed a storm, he raised the dead, he cast out demons, he turned water into wine, and he healed the sick. While these miracles stand alone as evidence of divine nature, the miracles also should be seen as communication vehicles that expressed the love, the authority, and the identity of one who is both the Son of God and God the Son. Miracles are the ultimate visual aid. In fact, Jesus clearly acknowledged that "the miracles I do in my Father's name speak for me" (John 10:25), and "Even though you do not believe me, believe the miracles, that you may know and understand that the Father is in me, and I in the Father" (John 10:38). Again, here in the Farewell Discourse, Jesus underscored this when he said, "Believe me when I say that I am in the Father and the Father is in me; or at least believe on the evidence of the miracles themselves" (John 14:11)

When the ancient Greeks spoke of rhetoric as using all the available means of persuasion, they referred to a somewhat different, if not overlapping, set of categories: *logos, pathos,* and *ethos.* Like the Socratic method, the Greek concept of rhetoric would have been well-known at the time of Christ in the Roman Empire. *Logos* is the content of the message. It is rightly translated "the word"—the essence of the message or propositional statement. Jesus is the *logos* of God—the whole of God's communication to his creation, for God did at times send messengers (prophets), but in the last days sent his Son (Hebrews 1) who not only proclaimed God's truth but was God's truth in human form. Of course, from the word *logos* we derive words like *logical* and *logo* in English. Communication of the *logos* appeals primarily to the left brain—sequential, rational, analytical, and objective.

Pathos appeals to the other side of the brain, which is more random, intuitive, synthesizing, and holistic. The word *pathos* contributed to English words such as *empathy, sympathetic,* and (if anyone cares) *apathy.* Stories, including many of the parables of Jesus, could be viewed as persuasion based on *pathos.* Drawing word pictures, creating mental images filled in by the listener, is a powerful communication vehicle because of the emotional appeal. Nathan the prophet appealed to King David's emotions to communicate to him God's wrath regarding his adultery with Bathsheba:

> The LORD sent Nathan to David. When he came to him, he said, "There were two men in a certain town, one rich and the other poor. The rich man had a very large number of sheep and cattle, but the poor man had nothing except one little ewe lamb he had bought. He raised it, and it grew up with him and his children. It shared his food, drank from his cup and even slept in his arms. It was like a daughter to him.
>
> "Now a traveler came to the rich man, but the rich man refrained from taking one of his own sheep or cattle to prepare a meal for the traveler who had come to him. Instead, he took the ewe lamb that belonged to the poor man and prepared it for the one who had come to him."
>
> *David burned with anger* against the man and said to Nathan, "As surely as the LORD lives, the man who did this deserves to die!" (2 Samuel 12:1–5, emphasis added).

There is great power in Nathan's story, whether it was fictional or based in fact. The great storytellers of our age have emerged and have demonstrated in our generation the power of the narrative—storytellers such as Garrison Keeler, Max Lucado, and even apologist Ravi Zacharias.

The third aspect of rhetoric is *ethos*, a term that proves to be somewhat challenging to define. It relates to the character of the communicator—in terms of character, perceived truthfulness, goodness. *Ethos* can include how well-liked a person is, his or her demeanor, appearance, and sense of humor. Although the etymology of ethics is traced back to *ethos*, *ethos* encompasses a whole range of subjective factors that affect credibility. (Recently I spoke at a conference along with a colleague from England, who was simply perceived as smarter or as more believable than me because of his British accent. That is the way it is on this side of the pond.) Jesus appealed to his *ethos*:

> Philip said, "Lord, show us the Father and that will be enough for us."
>
> Jesus answered: "Don't you know me, Philip, even after I have been among you such a long time? Anyone who has seen me has seen the Father. How can you say, 'Show us the Father'? Don't you believe that I am in the Father, and that the Father is in me? The words I say to you are not just my own. Rather, it is the Father, living in me, who is doing his work. Believe me when I say that I am in the Father and the Father is in me; or at least believe on the evidence of the miracles themselves (John 14:8–11).

Jesus readily invited people to believe his message based on his miracles (v. 11). But he was also equally prepared to invite people to believe based on his character.

It is not a reach to suggest that Jesus used all the available means of communication and persuasion—stories, demonstrations of his divinity, propositional teaching, Socratic dialogues—and that those various communications drew on the nature of the *logos* (the propositional teaching), the *pathos* (the stories) and his *ethos* (his sinless, divine character). Jesus' mastery of rhetoric is important. He was not one dimensional. While viewed from a human perspective, Jesus utilized all the available means of persuasion, means that appeal to both left- and right-brain orientations. When the *logos*, the word of God, comes to us, it comes fully orbed, not just communicating truth but conveying truth, and not just conveying truth but incarnating truth: "The Word [logos] became flesh and made his dwelling among us. . . . full of grace and truth" (John 1:14).

It should come as no surprise that the Creator of the universe should communicate in many creative ways (in addition to creation itself, which declares his praise[1]), and that his truth should be woven into the very fabric of human experience and world history. Harvard law professor William Stuntz (who was dying of cancer) wrote:

> Philosophers and scientists and law professors (my line of work) are not in the best position to understand the Christian story. Musicians and painters and writers of fiction are much better situated—because the Christian story is a *story*, not a theory or an argument, and definitely not a moral or legal code. Our faith is, to use C. S. Lewis's apt words, the myth that became fact. Our faith is a painting so captivating that you cannot take your eyes off it. Our faith is a love song so achingly beautiful that you weep each time you hear it. At the center of that true myth, that painting, that song stands a God who does vastly more than remember his image in us. He pursues us as lovers pursue one another. It sounds too good to be true, and yet it *is* true. So I have found, in the midst of pain and heartache and cancer.[2]

A BALANCED UNDERSTANDING OF TRUTH

If we are to have any hope of moving through a time of crisis in our lives, we must have a strong grip on the truth in all its expressions—the anchor that Paul called "the sword of the Spirit, which is the word of God" (Ephesians 6:17). It is perhaps worth noting that early in church history, the sword and the anchor (along with the fish) were prominent Christian symbols, long before the cross became the ubiquitous symbol of the faith. In some ways, if we squint our eyes a bit, a sword pointed up and an anchor even could resemble each other. Truth—the sword of the spirit—is our anchor. Yet the truth of God's Word must be seen as multidimensional if we recognize that "in the past God spoke to our forefathers through the prophets *at many times and in various ways,* but in these last days he has spoken to us by his Son" (Hebrews 1:1–2, emphasis added) and that Jesus himself communicated in various ways also. So in times of crisis, we need not only the propositional truth of God's Word—its *logos* of promises and proclamation—but we also need its poetry full of pathos and the stories of those who have gone on before; and we need to embrace the ethos of the person of the God-Man.

As a preacher and student of preaching, I have observed the trends throughout history of homiletics and hermeneutics, the interpretation and proclamation of God's Word. The early church divided on how the Word of God should be interpreted. The church fathers of the Latin West (Augustine, Ambrose, Jerome, and Gregory) sought what they perceived to be a deeper, allegorical meaning to the text, while the fathers of the Eastern Greek church (Athanasius, Basil, Gregory of Nazianzus, and John Chrysostom) sought a more literal understanding of the biblical text. The pendulum today seems to be moving away from an emphasis on verse-by-verse exposition of the Bible—with its roots in Greek thought (note that Paul, a favorite of didactic expositors, was trained in Tarsus, a center of Greek learning)—and toward an emphasis on narrative (with room for a shift to a broader hermeneutic, if not an allegorical one).

This shift may reflect a movement away from the head to the heart, or the cerebral to the emotive, or left brain to right brain. It may reflect a growing influence of 20th century existentialism. Or it may also reflect what some perceive as a pushback against the arrogance of evangelicals during the "battle for the Bible" era (the 1970s), a time when evangelical scholarship was entrenched in a very narrowly focused hermeneutic or understanding of God's Word.[3] Even well-known expositor Charles Swindoll argues that the best in exposition must still be wrapped in a story. Proposition without a connection to life expressed in a story or example is wooden or flat.

Jesus knew that. John Stott called it bridging between two worlds—the world of the biblical text with the world we live in.

The classical verse-by-verse or paragraph-by-paragraph exposition dominated the evangelical church for most of the last century, following a century of textual preaching[4] that expanded single phrases into entire sermons based on elaborate invention. The emphasis on the teaching of didactic passages, by my observation, has led to a disproportionate emphasis on the Pauline epistles to the neglect of the narratives of the New and especially the Old Testaments. Paul's writings are apparently easier to preach from than Hosea, even though Paul wrote that "All Scripture is God-breathed and is useful . . ." (2 Timothy 3:16)—and even though Peter suggested some things Paul wrote were difficult to understand (2 Peter 3:15–16).

While topical preaching—preaching that develops a selected topic from a variety of biblical texts—has never gone away, there has been in the past twenty-five years a new wave of topical preaching that seeks to attract listeners by focusing on "hot topics" that are perceived to be relevant. A recent door hanger from a church in my neighborhood listed an upcoming sermon series on addiction, depression, and anxiety. I wondered how many people would attend in response to each one thousand door hangers, and my suspicion is not many—but certainly no less than a flier that advertized a sermon series on 2 Thessalonians. One of the most consistently effective pastors in all of the United States that I know sees dozens of professions of faith each week in response to his predominately topical approach to preaching.

Add to the mix the new emphasis of the emergent church on narrative, both preaching from the narratives of Scripture and the extensive use of illustrative narratives as well. However, there is an undercurrent in the emergent movement of a disdain for the exposition of Scripture because it is perceived to be prescriptive and contrary to the spirit of discovery (self-discovery) and the place of discourse.

Sadly, this undercurrent seems to be flavored at times by a denigration of biblical truth with some implying, along with the zeitgeist, that there is no objective or correspondent truth. Rather, truth is subjectified. Paralleling the existentialism of twentieth century, truth has become a matter of individual exploration, personal discovery, and (unfortunately) subjective validation.

Not to be overlooked in the current milieu are those who use a Veg-O-Matic approach to the Bible, slicing and dicing and taking for themselves only the parts they find edible. While serving as vice president of the National Association of Evangelicals, I had the opportunity to debate on national television Bishop Vicky Gene Robinson, then the newly elected bishop of New Hampshire.[5] Robinson's election shook many and might ultimately lead to the breakup of the Episcopal Church USA, because he is a homosexual who left his wife and daughters for a man he has lived with for nearly twenty years. Robinson is a bishop, complete with crimson shirt and Roman collar. The Bible is wrong, assert Robinson and his compatriots, when it comes to homosexuality. Genesis 19, Leviticus 18 and 20, and Romans 1 have all been wrongly interpreted, they insist. The sin of Sodom and Gomorrah was a lack of hospitality, not that the male population wanted and nearly rioted in order to have sex with Lot's handsome male houseguests (Genesis 19:1–9). Paul, he posits, didn't mean what he said because he didn't understand the difference between homosexual orientation and homosexual behavior. Yet during his installation as bishop, the new bishop declared his belief that the Bible is the Word of God and contains "all things necessary to salvation"; and he pledged to "conform to the doctrine of the Episcopal Church."[6] Amazing! It seems only by postmodernism's denial of the law of noncontradiction that a person can claim to believe all the Bible says about salvation and at the same time reject what is says about sexuality. Behind this Scripture twisting is a man of the cloth who has embraced both literary deconstruction and intentional fallacy, products of postmodernism.[7]

So if we are to have any hope of moving through a time of crisis in our lives, we must have a strong grip on the truth, the sword of the Spirit, the Word of God. That is no easy task in a turbulent church culture.

Perspectives of a Homiletics Professor

Brian Lowery of *Preaching Today* in January 2009 clicked on the Google Trends website to see what people were logging onto. The list for that day was startling, for at the top of the list that week was John 3:16. It was the number-one search target because millions of people had recently watched the college football national championship game in which the Florida quarterback, Tim Tebow, had been shown with eye-black patches with "John" under the right eye and "3:16" under the left. People who had no idea what John 3:16 referred to generated millions of Internet hits.[8] Biblical illiteracy is rampant in the culture.

But more importantly, biblical illiteracy in the *church* is skyrocketing and now approaching what many consider a crisis.[9] The Barna Group reported, "The Christian body in America is immersed in a crisis of biblical illiteracy. . . . How else can you describe matters when most churchgoing adults reject the accuracy of the Bible, reject the existence of Satan, claim that Jesus sinned, see no need to evangelize, believe that good works are one of the keys to persuading God to forgive their sins, and describe their commitment to Christianity as moderate or even less firm?"[10]

Many churches have abandoned the systematic teaching in traditional Sunday school settings for adults, leaving many regular attendees biblically illiterate. My friend and former professor David Wells wrote that the evangelical church has "cheerfully plunged into astounding theological illiteracy."[11] Millions of Americans who declare themselves to be Christians "contend that Jesus was just like the rest of us when it comes to temptation—fallen, guilty, impure, and Himself in need of a savior."[12]

How can Jesus bring us through times of crisis if we don't have a firm grip on him as he is revealed in God's Word? The Navigators have long used the word-hand illustration to teach how we are to grasp the Word of God: the four fingers of the hand on one side of a Bible with the thumb grasping the Bible from the underside. The fingers are labeled in progression *Hearing, Reading, Study and Apply,* and *Memorize,* while the thumb is labeled *Meditate.* Millions have learned the word-hand way of grabbing hold of God's Word and have benefited from the illustration and the concepts that it teaches. This is good instruction if we are going to get a firm grip on the anchor of God's Word. While the Navigators have helped many to clasp the Word of God, there are growing numbers of Christians today who have no systematic technique for infusing the truth of God's Word into their lives; consequently, they have a weak grip on this critical anchor.

As one thoroughly committed to expositional preaching, I am tempted at this juncture to line up the pundits who will claim that all we need is a return to verse-by-verse preaching in our pulpits. Would that it were so simple! A very brief critique of preaching against the background of the contemporary environment might reveal some important insights.

First, verse by verse exposition of Scripture is for those who have been trained to eat solid food, the ranks of whom have been significantly diminished. While many need just that, they have no appetite for such preaching. The culture, with its short, television-conditioned attention span, has shaped both the churched and the unchurched as well. Some pastors perceive they face a lose-lose scenario: preach what people want to hear or preach to empty pews. The exodus from pastoral ministry of eighteen thousand pastors per year suggests in part that many simply don't know how to bridge the gap between the world and the Word.

Second, the existentialism of the twentieth century is bearing a harvest as well. The emphasis on therapeutic, topical preaching is to some degree understandable; it serves as a shortcut for those not prepared to take a firm grasp of the Word of God on their own but increasingly needy of its distilled counsel in an increasingly complex culture. Topical preaching may be an effective hook to bring un-churched people into church, and the data may support that in part. But the dilemma is that if all we ever teach is topical, needs-based messages, then we are left with lifelong spiritual infants who never learn to eat spiritual meat.

The third trend is toward narrative for the sake of narrative. The emergent church is a strong advocate of the use of narrative—both narrative preaching and preaching from the narratives of Scripture. Certainly the narratives are part of the whole counsel of God. Unfortunately, the emphasis on narrative may be rooted for some in a postmodern bias against truth expressed as proposition. Some appear to advocate the strong use of narrative so that listeners can determine "their own truth" and not be subjected to someone else's imposed ab-solute truth. Indeed, the culture is so strongly biased toward stories as a way of communicating truth and away from propositional truth that I even heard Lee Strobel acknowledge that his newest book, *The Case for Christ*, had to be couched as a story if he wanted anyone in the postmodern era to engage with it.

Certainly, the great challenge of the twenty-first century will be to learn again how to preach as Jesus did—uncompromising with the truth but nuanced to the culture and utilizing "all the available means of persuasion." No small challenge. If God's people are to have a firm grasp on God's Word, we must do more than entertain with good stories. Certainly, Jesus told good stories—parables and true stories—and preached both topically as well as expositionally (see

Luke 4:18ff), as was the custom of the synagogue.

There are two important channels for narratives. First, all preaching (expositional and topical) needs to be abundantly infused with stories that powerfully illustrate biblical truth. Biblical truth is illuminated by good stories, and the demand for good stories among good preachers is undiminished. "Hey! That will preach!" is the supreme compliment one preacher can pay to another's illustration. Sometimes we can move from the biblical truth to a story in a deductive pattern, and sometimes we can move from a story to a biblical truth in an inductive way. Jesus told many stories—it was an essential part of his preaching ministry—and used them both deductively and inductively. Just as we should not be surprised that apologist Lee Strobel has taken a narrative approach for his latest book, we should not be surprised that another world-class apologist, Ravi Zacharias, excels as a storyteller.

Second, preaching narrative passages from the Old and New Testaments is critical to proper balance that insures that the whole counsel of God is presented to God's people. This is no small thing, because preaching from narratives, especially Old Testament narratives, is challenging and demands great skill and the investment of time to be effective. Preaching from the epistles can be much easier, almost appearing as a default setting for some.

GUARDRAILS FOR TRUTH

God is a creative, relational being who has communicated to people in many ways and has preserved an historical account of those interactions in his Word. That Jesus is both the Word of God—an instrument of God's revelation—and the central focus of the Word of God in written form only demonstrates the centrality and finality of the Word. Within that biblical record we find a number of different literary genres: religious history, political history or annals, poetry and odes, proverbs and epigrams, prayers, songs of various kinds, genealogies, sermons, letters of all sorts, apocalyptic prophecy, and of course a great deal of biographical material concerning the Bible's central figure—the one who is the epitome of God's revelation, the Word made flesh.

Because God communicates truth in many ways, we ought to seek to communicate with all the available means as well—argumentation, illustration, storytelling, drama, poetry, pantomime, PowerPoint, visual arts, topical preaching, and (of course) expositional preaching. Didactic teaching and expository preaching are essential parts of the mix because they serve to crystallize our understanding of the truth, in much the same way that, according to Hebrews 1, Jesus crystallized all the revelation of God. "In the past God spoke to our forefathers through the prophets *at many times and in various ways*, but in these last days *he has spoken to us by his Son*, whom he appointed heir of all things, and through whom he made the universe. The Son is the radiance of God's glory and the exact representation of his being, sustaining all things by his powerful word" (vv. 1–3, emphasis added).

But although Jesus utilized all the available means of persuasion, he specifically used propositional teaching of the truth in a critical way. Recall what John recorded of the transaction between Jesus and the Eleven: "Though I have been speaking figuratively, a time is coming when I will no longer use this kind of language but will tell you plainly about my Father" (John 16:25). Then Jesus' disciples said, "Now you are speaking clearly and without figures of speech" (v. 29).

When the day was done, Jesus completed his teaching of God's truth to them, moving from figures of speech (parables and stories) to speaking "plainly" about his Father. Because figures of speech may be ambiguous (even intentionally, as we noted), Jesus wrapped up the discourse with propositional truth to eliminate any ambiguity. It is also clear that his declarations here brought the disciples to proclaim that they believed: "Now we can see that you know all things and that you do not even need to have anyone ask you questions. This makes us believe that you came from God" (16:30). This was a declaration established on Jesus' propositional teaching.

John recorded three propositions concerning the nature of truth and faith at the end of the discourse that Jesus made to his disciples. In summary:

- God does speak in a variety of ways, including figuratively, but he also speaks plainly in propositional statements that are essential.

- Jesus conveyed that there is a minimum of what we must believe in order to belong to Jesus in a significant way (it would appear that questions of eternal destiny are significant).

- The account in John affirms that everything we need to know about true religion is found in Jesus.

BARE MINIMUM OF TRUTH

What we are defending, of course, is a meaningful gospel, the nucleus of which is Jesus' propositional truth which we have received and on which we now stand (1 Corinthians 15:1). Without a meaningful gospel the church is rendered irrelevant and not worthy of anyone's time or effort or investment. Throughout history—and even before the dreaded modernist era—the church captured the propositional truths of the gospel as creeds; the Apostles' Creed and the Nicene Creed are the best known.

As we capture and highlight seven propositions that Jesus reiterated that night, note what he said: "A time is coming when I will no longer use this kind of language *but will tell you plainly about my Father*. . . . No, the Father himself loves you because you have loved me and have believed *that I came from God*. I came from the Father and entered the world; now I am leaving the world and *going back to the Father*" (John 16:25–28, emphasis added).

Jesus made a number of claims that would be classified as clear declarations of the truth:

- Jesus is the way, the truth, and the life.
- No one can find eternal life apart from faith in Jesus.
- Jesus came from God and was returning to God.
- God has put all things under Jesus' authority.
- Jesus would prepare an eternal home for those who belong to him.
- Jesus and Father are one.
- To see Jesus is to see the Father.

These truths are the nucleus of the gospel. These truths must be embraced in order to enter into a relationship of love with God through Jesus. There is no simple transaction to come to such a faith. Faith involves three distinct but related aspects: *notitia*, *assensus*, and *fiducia*. *Notitia* is the content of faith—the essence of the propositions themselves. *Assensus* refers to the intellectual aspect of faith—giving intellectual assent to the propositions and their meaning or significance. *Fiducia* (from which we get *fiduciary*) refers to the process of trusting.

In *The Flight of the Phoenix*, a cargo plane with several passengers crash-lands in the Sahara desert. The hope of rescue is remote and the situation seems hopeless. One passenger has aeronautical training but has only worked with model airplanes. His ambitious plan, to build a workable airplane out of the parts of the crashed plane, becomes the central question of faith for the movie. The tension builds as the passengers assemble the craft. The principles of flight, they are told, are the same, regardless of the size of the airplane—gravity, lift, thrust, and drag. They dismantle the damaged portions of the airplane and begin to construct a smaller and vastly different airplane from the usable parts—one engine instead of two, patched up wings, and limited control surfaces. Neither aviation theory nor the aircraft they patched together would take them home unless they were willing to take the ride of their lives—and possibly the last ride of their lives. There was content to their faith. An intellectual assent took them through the construction phase. Trust was needed to get in the plane, start the engine, and pull back on the throttle. All three parts were necessary for them to get home. Faith in faith is inadequate—that is mere fideism. Faith in the wrong object is inadequate, no matter how well we buckle our seat belts for the ride.

ATTACKS ON OUR ANCHOR

A relentless series of attacks on the truth of the Word of God are seen throughout history. These attacks threaten to erode or sever the ropes tied to the anchors that God provides for us. The attacks began in the garden of Eden when the tempter challenged Eve and her grasp of God's revelation: "'Did God really say, "You must not eat from any tree in the garden"?' . . . 'You will not surely die,' the serpent said to the woman. 'For God knows that when you eat of it your eyes will be opened, and you will be like God, knowing good and evil'" (Genesis 3:1–5).

In more recent history, the attacks on the inspiration (divine origin) and authority of God's Word have been renewed in every generation. Baruch (Benedict) Spinoza was the not the first modern critic of the Scriptures; but he was perhaps one of the most important; he seems to have galvanized the modern movement. A Hebrew scholar, he launched a vigorous challenge to the Mosaic authorship of the Pentateuch. Spinoza believed that these books, in fact the whole of the Old Testament, were composed by a limited number of historians living many generations after the events narrated. Consequently, he said, the Old Testament is not a record of God's revelation to us but a collection of stories about a nomadic tribal people who remarkably developed their own monotheistic religion quite apart from their polytheistic neighbors. Jews thought him a traitor to his people, Christians thought him a devil, and even the heretics of his day condemned him.

The reason the heretics of the day didn't embrace Spinoza was in great part due to his linguistic manipulations. Spinoza employed many of the same terms prevalent in traditional Jewish and Christian discourse, such as *salvation, faith, miracles, divine law, election,* and even *God,* but clearly twisted the words and ascribed to them unorthodox meanings, "part of his persuasive programme [sic], attempting to bring others around to his own point of view through the use of familiar terms. . . . Spinoza is busy 'doing things with words.'"[13]

Spinoza served, of course, as the foundation for the "documentary hypothesis" that the Old Testament was not written as ascribed but came from oral traditions passed down through generations and continually embellished and exaggerated. This is said to explain the supernatural elements of the Bible. The JEPD traditions (Jehovist, Elohist, Priestly, and Deuteronomist traditions) are distinct, sometimes conflicting, and can each be traced through the Scriptures.[14]

Attacks on the New Testament were certainly not far behind, coming in three waves. In the last century and a half there have been three so-called quests for the historical Jesus. The first quest began in the nineteenth century when David Friedrich Strauss published a book titled *Das Leben Jesu* (*The Life of Jesus*). Believing "that the Gospels could no longer be read straightforwardly as unvarnished historical records of what Jesus actually said and did," Strauss argued that new "unbiased" historical research needed to be done to find out who Jesus really was.[15] Because the Gospels and the life of the "old-fashioned Jesus" are so full of the supernatural (indeed, rooted in it), the Gospels were no longer regarded as historically trustworthy.

In the 1940s a second quest began with students of German theologian Rudolf Bultmann, who wrote that perhaps as little as 3 percent of the Gospels could be considered historical.[16] The "demythologizing" of the Scriptures proposed by Bultmann has known almost no bounds, as demonstrated by the third wave. The Jesus Seminar was launched in 1985 by Robert W. Funk as a forum for

NAVIGATING YOUR PERFECT STORM

"international debate about the 'historical Jesus'—that is, the real facts about the person to whom various Christian gospels refer."[17] Over the past twenty years, the Jesus Seminar has taken votes to determine what in the Gospels is authentic and what is not.

This short historical survey is not intended as a springboard to a lengthy, or even brief, refutation of those outside the scope of historic orthodoxy, but only to suggest that keeping a firm grip on the truth of God's Word is met with challenges from the non-Christian world that seek to unravel the cords holding our third anchor.

ATTACKS OF SABOTEURS

But there are growing challenges to the veracity of God's Word—subtle but very dangerous—now coming from within the ranks of evangelicalism as well. Some of it comes from the emergent church. And while there is much to commend the emergent church—its focus on community and missional living—there are some who have abandoned the Bible as the God-breathed revelation to man.

THE POST-MODERN EMERGENTS

First, under the premise of making the gospel "safe" for the postmodern world, certain streams of the emergent church disavow the propositional statements of the Bible because postmodernism disavows propositional truth. Truth, we are told by the postmodernist, is the product of, and therefore defined by, each culture. All truths are equal and cannot be hierarchical. Propositional statements and propositional truth are based on the correspondence theory of truth—that truth relates to an objective reality. Yet some in the emergent movement have repudiated propositional truth and even the correspondence theory of truth—the bedrock of the Christian faith—because they have embraced postmodernism.[18] Jeremy Green challenged Brian McLaren's overly generous orthodoxy: "God has revealed himself personally in Christ, but propositionally in Scripture as well. Propositional revelation is valuable because it can then be judged true or false according to how it corresponds to reality. Yet for McLaren, correspondence to objective reality is not a necessary condition for truth—truth is merely better opinion."[19]

But it is difficult to see how a "generous orthodoxy" that makes no absolute claim on objective truth, could in fact not be relativism. How is relativism not the logical entailment of this entire philosophical and theological construct? Some in the emergent church call us to be missional communities, but what is the mission? Certainly, it is not to send missionaries to other languages, tribes, peoples, and nations. If Hinduism and Islam and Mormonism are equally valid paths on the God-ward journey for sincere spiritual seekers, then we have crossed over the threshold into universalism. By all means, then, let's bring home all the missionaries. Judas Iscariot was right—there is no reason to spend money that could be given to the poor for the chauvinistic purpose of bringing unique honor to Jesus. And, if the Word made flesh really didn't leave us propositional truth, then, to the joy of the postmodern world, Christians must cease their offensive and condescending proselytizing because we have nothing in terms of truth to give to anyone.

If there is no propositional truth, then what is the church? McLaren suggested that the church will be a missional community committed to an "orthodoxy," but if it is merely a community that will continue "'reaching new and better conclusions' . . . to seek continually new ways to think about God,"[20] then the anchor has been cut, and the church is cast adrift. If Jesus is the way, the truth, and the life, the complete revelation of God (John 14; Hebrews 1), then what new ways should we think about God? Certainly we don't know all there is to know about God (Isaiah 55:8). However, if the primary mission of the church is to gather people to share their theological opinions in order to find new ways to think about God without the anchor of God's propositional truth, we have all been cast adrift.

Such a gathering has no prophetic voice, just opinions, informed and uninformed.

Propositional statements of truth provide guardrails for those seeking to keep a vital, firm grip on the Word of God. Orthodoxy becomes heterodoxy and potentially heresy when it argues that the Bible is merely a collection of narratives of God's interactions with a specific tribe of ancient people couched in phenomenological language that have no direct relevance to anyone other than the Hebrews. We are left with an empty shell of a religion where no objective truth about God can be known. Christianity is reduced to one of many options among the religions of the world if its central propositions are leeched of their truth and authority in a relativistic marketplace of ideas. While the various genres of biblical literature all contribute to our understanding of God, it is the propositional truths that are essential for interpreting the figurative portions and for codifying our essential doctrines. If the propositional teaching of Jesus—which John recorded in chapters 13–16—is to be regarded as unreliable, mythological, or arrogant hierarchical truth, then historic Christianity has been totally co-opted by the doctrines of the Jesus Seminar, Bultmann's demythologizing, and the postmodern philosophy of the day. Orthodoxy has become heterodoxy.

Doing theology without the guardrails provided by propositional truth leads to aberrant theology, as we track the devolution of the emergent movement's iconic radical. Early writings by Brian McLaren are engaging insights about the flaws of the church of the 20th century, but in *Everything Must Change* he sought to dismantle and then reconstruct historic orthodoxy into something that was more to his liking and which remarkably resembles the social gospel of a century ago: "Christ's cross work was not for the purpose of propitiating divine wrath or redemption from sin; it was a nonviolent example for us to follow"; "the second coming of Christ is without biblical warrant"; and "a new heaven and earth are unnecessary because 'good will prevail by peace, love, truth, faithfulness, and courageous endurance of suffering.'"[21] And in his most recent work, *A New Kind of Christianity*, McLaren seems to have run completely off the track—Brian may have left the building! He has moved beyond trashing evangelicalism—his hobbyhorse—to dismantling the God of the Bible, rendering the eternal God to be little more than the secular anthropologists' idea that God (monotheism) is the end product of a process of religious evolution.[22] When we reject propositional truth as the foundation of our faith and remove the guardrails, this is where we end up. Augustine was correct: "If you believe what you like in the Gospels, and reject what you don't like, it is not the gospel you believe, but yourself."[23]

Recently a friend related an interaction with a Mormon bishop who is part of a men's small-group Bible study. The bishop said that he was growing in his faith and was "more in love with Jesus than ever." I understand why my friend found that exciting, but I was not quite so hopeful. Some today would argue that people of other faiths can become followers of Christ without leaving their native worldview and that sometimes it may even be beneficial to stay in that worldview. The difference between the Jesus of the New Testament orthodoxy is light years from the Jesus of Mormonism. We have two very different, incompatible, and irreconcilable worldviews. In one worldview there is a God who eternally exists in three persons—Father, Son, and Spirit—and who created all things, visible and invisible. In the other, there is the quasi divine Son of God who was once man and became God, holding out the opportunity for each person to become a god and rule his own universe by following the example of Jesus.

So which Jesus is the bishop in love with? Is it the Jesus of the Jesus Seminar, stripped of his deity and rendered the spiritual equivalent of a prune? Or is it the Jesus who still comfortably fits within the heretical teaching of the Church of Jesus Christ of the Latter Day

Saints? Is he the son of God, as we are all sons of God, according to Mormon doctrine? Or is he God the Son, the eternally self-existent God in human form? If it's only about the direction and sincerity of the journey and not the destination, then we could all get excited about the faith of those who can claim to love their Jesus without coming to grips with the propositional teaching of the Bible.

This bishop may yet come to faith in the unfiltered Jesus through the work of the Holy Spirit who can guide him into all truth, but that will require loving the Jesus of the New Testament enough to sort through the Mormon word games.

LINGUISTIC DECONSTRUCTIONISTS

The second subtle attack on the truth of God's Word comes from the penchant of postmoderns to deconstruct language and render all propositional statements impotent—much like Baruch Spinoza who was "doing things with words." The postmodernists suggest that words have no objective referent, so the only meaning of a message is that assigned by the reader or listener. Michel Foucault argued that communication was always an attempt by the communicator to oppress the hearer or reader. To rectify that, the listener deconstructs the message and assigns a subjective meaning. What the author intended is irrelevant.[24] It comes as little surprise that Nietzsche—a taproot of postmodernism and a pioneer in the deconstruction of language—argued, "I am afraid we are not rid of God because we still have faith in grammar."[25]

There is an objective nature to the Word of God. "Thus says the Lord" is repeated more than 750 times in the Bible for a reason. Our God is a communicative God, and in the fullness of time the Word became flesh—the ultimate objectification of God's word to us. So our diligence concerning language is critical, lest we surrender to the subtle popularizations of Lewis Carroll—another precursor to deconstructionism—and his Wonderland characters. There, words have no conventional meaning and mean whatever the speaker deems them to mean.[26]

There is an urgent need today to reaffirm the sanctity of God's Word because its authority is under renewed attack, even from within the general confines of the church. The uncritical acceptance within mainstream evangelicalism of postmodernism, which deconstructs and reconstructs either language or propositional truth, serves as a further warning that the perceived integrity of God's Word and its careful use are at risk. (Read my article on the intentional fallacy, "Standing for the Truth on Two Hills," in Appendix 2.)

WELL MEANING EVANGELICALS

The third subtle subversion of the truth of God's Word comes from well-intended Christian authors whose writings have been embraced uncritically in place of the Word. Among these are books of fiction that have seemingly become the foundation of doctrine in some clusters. *The Shack* has been a publishing phenomenon and has helped many think about God and their perceptions of God. Yet there is great danger in building our understanding of the incomprehensible concept of the Trinity on the portrait painted in the book. A black woman as God the Father and a Tinkerbell-like Holy Spirit are not helpful to everyone, however. Similarly, a number of years ago Frank Peretti wrote *Piercing the Darkness*, an engaging novel about spiritual warfare. A generation later it appears that much of what Peretti wrote about demons and angels has been adopted by evangelical Christians as truth, even though the Bible is silent on many of these points. They base their doctrine of demons and angels not on the Word of God but on a novel.

A wave of understandable enthusiasm among men for the recent *Wild at Heart* movement confronts us with another subtle subversion of the truth of God's Word. It appears to many that the well-meaning strategy to revitalize true masculinity in the North American church

NAVIGATING YOUR PERFECT STORM

has been based more on the *Braveheart* model for masculinity than the Word of God. The theological result has been sloppy at best and deceptive at worst—and, in either case, scary.

> Eve was created within the lush beauty of Eden's garden. But Adam, if you'll remember, was created *outside* the Garden, in the wilderness. In the record of our beginnings, the second chapter of Genesis makes it clear: Man was born in the outback, from the untamed part of creation. Only afterward is he brought to Eden. And ever since then . . . men have had an insatiable longing to explore. We long to return; it's when most men come alive. . . . The core of a man's heart is undomesticated *and that is good.*[27]

Good? I question how such a universalization squares with reality and with God's Word. I'm a somewhat bookish man who likes to cook, not just barbecue. I have a denim shirt, but I do not aspire to the great outdoors, let alone hunting and fishing, four wheeling, or mountain biking. But it is the questionable use of Scripture woven through the teaching of the movement that has caused the alarm to go off in the minds of many:

> The entirety of *Wild at Heart* flows from this faulty understanding of Eden. A proper reading of Genesis 2 turns [John] Eldredge's thesis on its head by revealing the true nature and purpose of Eden—thus helping to ensure a biblical view of manhood. Eden not only pictures the perfect fellowship between God and man before sin entered the world, it is also typological throughout redemptive history. . . .
>
> Eldredge's statement that a man's heart "can only be found through the help of wilderness" (p. 3), is confusing at best and unbiblical at worst.[28]

To a generation of the church that is already getting low grades for biblical literacy, such a line of thought is dangerous. Many men have uncritically embraced a wild at heart theology, resulting in anecdotal evidence that a number of men have left their wives and families to follow their wild hearts.

I have been averse to mentioning Brian McLaren and others by name, but I find it difficult to be veiled in my observations because Brian, especially, is so well known; because he is for many the poster child of the postmodernist emergent movement; because I like Brian; and because I really cannot judge the content of his heart. But, there is more to it. My post-modern friends with whom I teach philosophy staunchly defend McLaren and tell me I am a Neanderthal from back in the 20th century who arrogantly holds to the ideas of propositional truth (which must be hierarchical) and the accompanying evangelical hermeneutics.

What they miss is that I *desperately* hold to this—not arrogantly, but as humbly as I can. I *desperately* hold to the idea the Bible contains propositional truth (as well as narrative et al) because I need to do so if I am ever going to find hope. I wrote to a colleague:

> And just a thought. If you were dying, would you find any comfort from Brian McLaren's ideology? There is no atonement for sin; Jesus was a moral example; there is no objective truth, so Jesus is not—indeed cannot be—the way, the truth, and the life. It matters little what you believe since all roads lead to God/Allah/Whomever, etc.
>
> And Paul was at least in one sense correct: *And if Christ has not been raised, our preaching is useless and so is your faith. More than that, we are then found to be false witnesses about God, for we have testified about God that he raised Christ from the dead. But he did not raise him if in fact the dead are not raised. For if the dead are not*

raised, then Christ has not been raised either. And if Christ has not been raised, your faith is futile; you are still in your sins. Then those also who have fallen asleep in Christ are lost. If only for this life we have hope in Christ, we are to be pitied more than all men (1 Corinthians 15).

Sounds a bit like propositional truth to me.

I'm dying. And I think about dying every day. I find no comfort in this post-modern recast of Orthodox Christianity. There is nothing generous about it. Perhaps you have found a message of hope in post-modernism that will provide me some hope. Orthodoxy. Doctrine. Truth. These matter if we are to have an anchor to our hope.

You post-moderns think that if someone disagrees with you it is because they must not be listening. Not so. Let's talk some more. I'm listening—for hope.

There have to be some guardrails or we enter the post-modern world where there really is no meaning to life and no hope beyond. In the post-modern world we are left with a rope to pull us through the perfect storm, but it is not tied to any anchor. The propositional truth—if nothing else the "great and precious promises"—of God's word are our anchor in life and in death.

Now at the end of the final meal Jesus shared with the disciples, we see men who were emotionally exhausted. An hour later while Jesus prayed, they were all found sleeping in the garden. Yet spiritually they were well! Never better, in fact, for Jesus had spoken plainly to them, not just in figurative language or with theological abstractions but finally in clear statements that crystallized all that he had taught them—and they had finally believed!

They had a firm grasp on the truth of God's Word, our third essential anchor for passing through a crisis. In the Word of God, we find declarations of God's love and care for those who belong to him as well as affirmations that God is in complete control regardless of the circumstances. These are our first two anchors. But the Bible offers more. It provides illustrations, examples, stories of how those first two anchors work in real life. We need go no further in the book of Genesis than the story of Joseph for a compelling narrative of God's covenantal relationship that shapes Joseph's identity and destiny as well as a story about God's remarkable control over all things. Joseph had the first two anchors to enable him to pass through the ordeals of betrayal, slavery, injustice, and prison. He did not have what we have—the completed written revelation of God's repeated demonstration and proclamation that we know as the true Word of God.

In light of the increasing attacks that would sever the cords to our third anchor, we must diligently maintain the integrity of our equipment. There has never been a time when we have needed to hold onto it more securely than now.

7
ANCHOR 4:
LEARNING TO PRAY AGAIN

UNTIL NOW YOU HAVE NOT ASKED FOR ANYTHING IN
MY NAME. ASK AND YOU WILL RECEIVE, AND YOUR
JOY WILL BE COMPLETE.

There are many books about prayer, and I greatly appreciate the
excellent contribution several have made to my prayer life. But
because my own meager prayer life would not qualify as a good model for any believer, I am very reluctant to write much about prayer
here except to make a handful of observations about prayer as the
important fourth anchor. This is the reason for the brevity of this
chapter.

Jesus told the disciples, "Until now you have not asked for anything in my name" (John 16:24). It is not as though the disciples
had not learned to pray before this. Jesus modeled prayer for them
regularly and often taught them about prayer:

- Do not pray like the pagans with endless babbling.
- Pray with persistence.
- Pray the disciples' prayer (the "Lord's Prayer").
- The Father knows your needs before you ask.

- Watch and pray regarding temptation.
- Go secretly into a private place to pray.
- Pray believing that God hears us.

Curiously, before this, Jesus had not suggested that the disciples pray in his name. The model prayer includes no such statement. But as they stood at the threshold of a whole new life era, Jesus instructed them to pray in his name—to ask the Father on behalf of the Son. When they walked out the door of the upper room—and especially when they walked out of another upper room about fifty days later on Pentecost—their world would be vastly different. They would have entered into a whole new realm of spiritual warfare. The evil one, whose heel had been bruised at the cross, would escalate the spiritual conflict as the church of Jesus Christ was established on Pentecost with the outpouring of the Holy Spirit.

THE NATURE OF PRAYER

I've greatly appreciated John Piper's insights about prayer and the reality of spiritual warfare encapsulated in a message more than twenty years ago:

> We must talk first about war. Because life is war. And it is utterly impossible for people to know what prayer really is until they know that they are in a war, and until they know that the stakes of that war are infinitely higher. . . .
>
> But most people do not believe this in their heart. . . . They believe we are in peacetime, not wartime. . . .
>
> [But] until people believe this, they will not pray as they ought. They will not even know what prayer is. . . .
>
> Prayer is the communication by which the weapons of warfare are deployed according to the will of God. Prayer is for war. . . .
>
> Prayer is for the accomplishment of a wartime

mission. It is as though the field commander (Jesus) called in the troops, gave them a crucial mission ("Go and bear fruit"), handed each of them a personal transmitter coded to the frequency of the general's headquarters, and said, "Comrades, the general . . . has authorized me to give each of you personal access to him through these transmitters. If you stay true to his mission and seek his victory first, he will always be as close as your transmitter, to give tactical advice and to send in air cover when you or your comrades need it."

But what have millions of Christians done? They have stopped believing that we are in a war. . . . And what did they do with the walkie-talkie? They tried to rig it up as an intercom in their cushy houses . . . not to call in fire power for conflict with a mortal enemy, but to ask the maid to bring another pillow to the den.[1]

Jesus told them in the upper room that a radical change was coming in regard to prayer: "I tell you the truth, my Father will give you whatever you ask in my name." Why will the Father give us what we ask in the name of Jesus? The answer is simple enough: he will do this if and when we are engaged in fulfilling the mission that Jesus gave us. If we return to an earlier moment in the evening, when Jesus was discussing the vine and branches, we will understand why: "You did not choose me, but I chose you and appointed you to go and bear fruit—fruit that will last. *Then the Father will give you whatever you ask in my name*" (John 15:16, emphasis added).

The process by which the Father will give us what we ask is directly linked to our appointment to go and bear fruit. The Father will give us what we need in order to accomplish this primary task of bearing lasting fruit for the kingdom of God. He will answer prayers in Jesus' name when we are fulfilling Jesus' mission—to help complete the purchase of people for God from every language and tribe and people and nation.

That does not mean that we cannot or should not ask God for what we need personally for our own existence and well-being. Jesus told us that the Father cares about those needs as well. We are, after all, more valuable than the birds of the air that he cares for, feeds, and clothes (Matthew 6:28–32). Paul instructed us, "Do not be anxious about anything, but in everything, by prayer and petition, with thanksgiving, present your requests to God" (Philippians 4:6). But as nontraditional or antitraditional as it may sound, it appears that we do not need to ask the Father in Jesus' name for the necessities of life. Of course, that is not to say we cannot or should not invoke the name of Jesus our High Priest at any time in our prayers, from giving thanks for a meal to the invocation at a high school graduation. But God has already promised separately to meet our needs—even apart from invoking Jesus' name and authority. Jesus had been instructing his disciples to do just that all along.

So it would appear that a special promise was to be inaugurated in the very near future (with Jesus' departure) for the disciples. In order to fulfill the mission—to bear lasting fruit, advance the kingdom, and complete the Great Commission—they were authorized to ask in Jesus' name and to have the assurance that the Father would answer those prayers.

This is clearly a refinement of the established teaching that if we ask in Jesus' name we can be certain that God will grant it. We have traditionally limited that promise by appending the words "according to his will." However, we may be more in keeping with this instruction to instead add "in order to bear lasting fruit for the kingdom." The use of Jesus' name and the resulting promise of the Father to answer add a previously unknown or untapped dimension of prayer: a special authority for the task of bearing fruit for God's kingdom.

Even a cursory study of Paul's statements on prayer reveals two similar categories about prayer. First, Paul prayed continually for the saints in all the churches. What he prayed for was their spiritual growth, their wisdom and understanding, their spiritual power, and their unity in the Spirit, and for their lives to be worthy of their calling—even as he thanked God for them and their progress. Paul's top prayer requests for himself were for his release from confinement to preach the Word (this keeps appearing and reappearing), for his preaching to bear fruit by the power of God, for new doors to be opened for the ministry, and for boldness and courage to proclaim the gospel as God gave him opportunity. There simply is little reference in Paul's correspondence to praying for physical or personal needs, not because those things didn't matter but because he presumed that God knew, cared, and could be trusted to provide: "He who did not spare his own Son, but gave him up for us all—how will he not also, along with him, graciously give us all things?" (Romans 8:32).

All of this suggests a higher echelon of prayer. Prayer in the midst of ongoing spiritual warfare for the advance of the kingdom has been given the highest priority at the throne of heaven. We have been given Jesus' name to invoke for prayer from the battlefield. Battlefield prayer is tactical. Prayer for rations and tents and gas for the Humvee are strategic prayers, which have a different priority level because the quartermaster knows from experience what supplies the troops need even before they send in their requisitions in triplicate on the proper form. But the tactical situation on the front lines is fluid and requires communication that reaches HQ directly. It is stamped with the name of the field commander who promised he will never leave nor forsake his troops. Make no mistake: battlefield communications have a unique and very special importance in the kingdom of God.

HOW PRAYER IS NURTURED

Prayer is hard work. C. S. Lewis wrote that the difficulty of prayer is that "by the very constitution of our minds as they now are . . . it is difficult for us to concentrate on anything which is neither sensible (like potatoes) nor abstract (like numbers). What is concrete but immaterial can be kept in view only by painful effort."[2] He calls prayer *irksome*, a word I doubt I have ever used in conjunction with prayer, but which adds a refreshingly honest assessment of our painful effort:

> The odd thing is that this reluctance to pray is not confined to periods of dryness. When yesterday's prayers were full of comfort and exaltation, today's will still be felt as, in some degree, a burden.
>
> Now the disquieting thing is not simply that we skimp and begrudge the duty of prayer. The really disquieting thing is that it should have to be numbered among duties at all. . . .
>
> If we were perfected, prayer would not be a duty, it would be delight. Some day, please God, it will be. . . .
>
> I must say my prayers today whether I feel devout or not; but that is only as I must learn my grammar if I am ever to read the poets.[3]

Prayer is a difficult discipline we must learn until it becomes second nature. The goal is to become people who pray constantly, "without ceasing," as Scripture says (1 Thessalonians 5:17 NASB). We must learn to pray, and to do so we must overcome three sources of this spiritual inertia of rest.

THINKING PRAYER MAKES NO DIFFERENCE

First, we must address the issue of belief. David Wells called us on this when he wrote that the reason we don't pray as we should is that we don't believe prayer will make any difference.[4] That is a significant indictment, yet it appears there are many who have come to that prayer-arresting conclusion. I think of my mother. Her husband, my father, whom I mentioned earlier, was sent home from the hospital to die of cancer at a fairly early age. She told me some years later that she had not really prayed in years. She recalled that she had prayed and fasted and fasted and prayed and that her husband died anyway. She said she had been unable to pray since his death because she didn't believe it would make any difference.

She is not alone in this crisis of faith; she and those like her need to see that God's goodness and faithfulness cannot be evaluated in terms of one unanswered prayer, however easy it is to arrive at such a conclusion. Paradoxically, it seems that God is most distant at times of crisis, calling on us to the principle of walking by faith and not by sight.

THINKING I AM SELF-SUFFICIENT

Second, we need to overcome the inertia of pride and the accompanying attitude of self-sufficiency. Jesus said resolutely, "I am the vine. You are the branches. . . . Apart from me you can do nothing" (John 15:5). We could live with that more easily if he had said, "Apart from me you can do some things, but connected to me you can do more things." It is humbling each day to ask for daily bread. It is humbling to have to pray each day for wisdom, guidance, grace, mercy, and peace. Isn't there some way we could "pray up for a week" and then coast? I find it humbling every day to acknowledge, "Father, I am a sinner in need of mercy. I am a created being, and you are the Creator. I am utterly dependent on your grace today for every breath I take, every beat of my heart, and every material need."

Well, I prayed that yesterday, I argue in my own proud self-sufficient heart. Do I really need to pray that again today? The humbling answer is yes! Although ritual prayers can be offered in advance with a Pharisee-like self-sufficiency, real prayer begins each day with a crucified pride.

NOT UNDERSTANDING OUR NEW-BIRTH RIGHT

Third, we need to overcome our guilt and shame. God loves us with a perfect and unchanging love, and he longs for us to come to him, to ask of him, to test and affirm his great and precious promises. He knows us intimately—our thoughts, our motives, our guilt, our shame; and he has made provision in Christ so that we can approach him regardless of our perceived condition. Hebrews 4:9–15 reveals a God who invites us to abandon our efforts of self-righteousness and sin management—and enter into his rest. He will search us with his Word (not always a comfortable process as we know) and reveal to us our true spiritual condition. He reminds us that regardless of our spiritual condition that we have a sympathetic High Priest who lives eternally to intercede for those he redeemed. He invites into his presence, into an environment of grace and mercy. His invitation to come *boldly* confirms that there is nothing that need keep us from prayer except our lack of understanding our spiritual new-birth right.

THE PROBLEM OF UNANSWERED PRAYER

While unanswered prayer might represent something especially difficult for the severely mistrusting person, we all need to wrestle to the ground the problem—sometimes the huge problem—of unanswered prayer. The promises of Jesus are disconcerting: "Whatever you ask for in prayer, believe that you have received it, and it will be yours" (Mark 11:24). In addition, Jesus told us that our heavenly Father, like our earthly fathers, longs to give good gifts to his children (Matthew 7:11). Unanswered prayer can be a huge stumbling block or even the rocks on which faith is shipwrecked. Broadcasting mogul Ted Turner said that he lost his faith when the tsunami of prayer offered up for his terminally ill brother yielded only frustration and ended in fatality. Unanswered pray left him cynical about Christianity.

So how shall we understand this?

How are we to understand the Holy Spirit as God's abundant

answer to our prayers—even those prayers that go "unanswered"? Margaret Manning, with some help from Craig Barnes, pointed to Jesus' provision of the fourth anchor for our lives, the Holy Spirit:

> First, what God promises to us through the answer of the Holy Spirit is the promise of God's presence with us in and through all the circumstances of life. The Bible speaks of the Holy Spirit as the comforter, the one who comes alongside of us. The promise of God's presence with us sustains us, even when God says "no" to our specific requests. Moreover, God is the answer to our prayers. As M. Craig Barnes, former pastor of the National Presbyterian Church in Washington, D.C. explains, "To receive Jesus as Savior means recognizing him as our only help. Not our only help for getting what we want. But our only true help."[5]

This "good gift" (Matthew 7:11), the Holy Spirit, hovered over the chaotic waters and created the world filled with beauty and blessing. This same good gift raised Jesus Christ from the dead and raises us to newness of life. The gift of the Holy Spirit is the depository of hope that we too can rise from the ashes of the most crushing events and circumstances. . . . "God longs to give to each one of us the supernatural power that comes from the indwelling presence of the Holy Spirit, today and in our lives right now!"[6]

Even as kedge anchors were used in tandem to negotiate a narrow anchorage, the anchors we have from Jesus are linked together. We have his words, his "great and precious promises" (2 Peter 1:4), and we have his Spirit, who guides us into all truth (John 16:13). And the link between them is prayer.

There is no single pathway of nurture for us to learn how to pray. But learn we must. Otherwise we risk encountering a crisis without having developed an adequate capacity for prayer and an intimacy with God. Of course we cannot exclude the possibility that God would allow or even bring a crisis to teach us how to pray if we have not learned earlier (a truth not easily processed by any of us). And it might well be that God will allow a crisis to teach us to pray as preparation for an even bigger crisis later. So the time to check the gauge or practice using a fire extinguisher is before the pan boils over and the kitchen starts to burn. The time to learn to pray is before we find ourselves in a major spiritual conflict. Learning how to pray is learning how to kedge! It is a skill best learned in still waters before a fleet of spiritual forces is in hot pursuit.

8

ANCHOR 5:
FOLLOWING OUR GUIDE

BUT WHEN HE, THE SPIRIT OF TRUTH, COMES, HE
WILL GUIDE YOU INTO ALL TRUTH.

For three years the disciples had lived with God, even though they did not fully comprehend this. They certainly saw glimpses of deity cloaked in humanity as they witnessed various miracles, from the feeding of the five thousand to the raising of the dead. Perhaps the miracle that reveals the most about the disciples' understanding of whose company they were keeping took place on the Sea of Galilee.

THE COMFORTER

Luke tells the story of the storm, the sleeping rabbi, and the calming of the tempest. However, Luke's account is curious in this regard: these professional fishermen panicked in the storm and did what they did best with their limited faith—they called on Jesus. After Jesus calmed the storm, we would expect to read that the disciples were greatly relieved. Instead, Luke says that they were "terrified."

Why were they terrified? Because they realized that day who was in the boat with them. The eternal Creator and sustainer of the universe was in the boat—with them! That reality suddenly proved more terrifying than the storm itself.

Although the disciples were terrified on those occasions when they were confronted by a glimpse of the fullness of Godhead in bodily form, they had actually become quite comfortable having the Son of God among them. He comforted them. He protected them. He provided for them. He paid their taxes for them from the mouths of fish. The Son of God had been with them, physically limited to one place in space and time. He was the presence of the God who said, "I will walk among you and be your God, and you will be my people" (Leviticus 26:12). He had dwelled (tented) with them around the countryside of Judea and Galilee—and boated with them on the Sea of Galilee. All of that was about to change.

What Jesus told the disciples about the Holy Spirit required a paradigm shift. No longer would the incarnate God be present with them in physical form; he would be with them spiritually in the form of the Holy Spirit of God, the same Spirit that indwelled Jesus. This was necessary for a very practical reason. As long as the church, the new family of God, was limited to eleven men and a few friends, it was possible for God the Son to be with them, protect them, provide for them, comfort them, and instruct them. As the church stood on the threshold of an explosive growth curve, the incarnate Son of God could not be with each of them, as they and thousands of others would be scattered all over the Roman Empire. The incarnation was severely limiting, and while the disciples experienced the physical presence of God the Son, they would soon need the unbounded presence of God the Spirit. This is why Jesus told them: "But I tell you the truth: It is for your good that I am going away. Unless I go away, the Counselor will not come to you; but if I go, I will send him to you" (John 16:7).

We can certainly understand why they are filled with grief, and much of their grief was inherently selfish (as is grief generally). While the church would gain the daily and ubiquitous presence of Christ by his Spirit, the disciples would lose his immediate physical presence with them, a presence they could not at that point imagine being without. It would prove to be a remarkable trade, completed on the day of Pentecost.

Jesus referred to the Holy Spirit here as the *parakletos*, the one who comes and stands alongside. The word picture is vivid and well-known. Jesus might have chosen it in order to convey the sameness of the era to come. He had been there, standing alongside the disciples. The Spirit would likewise come and be with them, standing alongside them. Jesus said that "another" comforter would come, as John recorded it, using the word that implies another of the same kind rather than another of a different kind.

In a deep personal crisis, Ed Landry experienced a profound presence of the *parakletos*:

> I was busy in ministry and conditioning my body in preparation for a trip to Nepal in October of this year. . . . But something was wrong with my body. I have always been fairly athletic and generally in good physical condition. But I began getting very tired doing even the simplest activity. A very good friend who is a doctor recognized that I was anemic and had me get some blood tests. The results suggested that I should immediately leave for the States for more conclusive tests.
>
> I arrived in Seattle seven weeks ago. The tests were run. Two days later I sat in the office of the head of oncology and hematology in one of the best cancer centers in the USA and was told I had acute myelogenous leukemia.
>
> I asked her to elaborate a bit about how bad this

was. She said that without treatment I would only live two months at best. She explained that I had probably had the disease about a month and that it is a very aggressive type of cancer in the bone marrow. Very few survive this particular form of the disease.

My first response to the doctor was, "Wow, two months. That's some disease." Then I said, "Bummer, I just got a haircut. I could have saved some money." Then I remarked, "You said I have acute myelogenous leukemia. Is that better than an ugly one?"

At this point she said, "Mr. Landry, this is not a joking matter." I said, "I thought it was a pretty good joke." All I can say at that point was that the presence of the Lord came very near.

"What you are telling me is not a big problem because to me death is not a big problem. I am a born-again Christian. It has been my greatest joy to serve my Lord in this way for many years. It will be an even greater joy when I go to Heaven and meet him face-to-face. For me life has been a wonderful adventure and if this is the last chapter, then it will be the best chapter and I look forward to every bit of it."

They just stared at me. I think I was supposed to faint or something and look sad, but I couldn't. I had such a peace inside that I couldn't contain sharing Christ with them. It was really wonderful.

I can't tell you every story, but I can summarize my first [full] month in the cancer ward of the hospital with the word *joy*. Deep and rich.

To the world it makes no sense. I was connected day and night to feeding tubes, had 18 blood transfusions, bone chips and marrow were taken from my hip three times, my spinal fluid was tapped, and chemo put in my spinal column. I was unable to eat anything for three weeks. All food was fed through tubes that had to be surgically implanted in my chest. My hair fell out and I was only able to sleep 2–3 hours a night for the entire month. How could that be a joyful experience? The Lord was present by my side all the time.

I woke up sometimes at night and it was like he was hugging me. Wouldn't you do that with your kids if they were sick? The night times were sometimes the best. Prayer was special, his presence was real, the Scriptures were so alive. It was pure joy. I can't even remember the pain. All I remember is the peace of heart.

We go back next Sunday to check into the hospital for the next season of joy. Pray with us as we return and find out what chapter he is writing.[1]

THE CONFRONTER

The second ministry of the Spirit would also parallel Jesus' ministry: "When he comes, he will convict the world of guilt in regard to sin and righteousness and judgment: in regard to sin, because men do not believe in me; in regard to righteousness, because I am going to the Father, where you can see me no longer; and in regard to judgment, because the prince of this world now stands condemned" (John 16:8–11).

In what may be one of the most pregnant passages of Scripture, Jesus told his little band of followers what the work of the Holy Spirit would be. Clearly, it would both complement and parallel the work that Jesus did on earth.

First, the Spirit would convict the world of guilt regarding sin. Apart from the convicting work of the Holy Spirit, we are doomed to remain as we are in our sin. Because we are dead in our sin, only the work of the Holy Spirit can enable us to become spiritually sensitive to our sin and our alienation from God. It is part of the process of regeneration. On our own we cannot and do not seek God and the forgiveness of sin that he offers through Christ. However, Jesus connected sin with disbelief because the ultimate sin is to disbelieve and reject the Son of God and the forgiveness he offers. The Holy Spirit would regenerate those who were dead in sin who had faith in Christ and his work on the cross.

Second, the Holy Spirit would impress on the disciples that Christ fully manifested the righteousness of God. Since Jesus was returning to the Father and his visible presence would not be in the world, the perfect righteousness of Jesus might fade from their minds or even be forgotten. Jesus' death on the cross was critical, but what made it effective on our behalf was his sinlessness. God made him, who knew no sin, to actually become and bear sin for us (2 Corinthians 5:21). One of the works of the Spirit is to keep the sinlessness of Jesus foremost in our minds. It is central to our salvation, but it is also central to our sanctification because the Spirit works to create in us the sinless character of Jesus.

The third work of the Holy Spirit is a bit more difficult to unpack here. The Spirit would convince and remind the world about the judgment—but what follows next should suggest to us that Jesus was not speaking of the final judgment of God. Instead, it appears that Jesus was speaking about the imminent judgment of the evil one, whom he called the prince of this world. His judgment would take place at the cross and through the resurrection when the power of death was overcome. A key to this understanding is found in John 12:31: "Now is the *time for judgment* on this world; now the prince of this world will be driven out" (emphasis added).

When Jesus spoke of the prince of the world being judged, he spoke of the usurped dominion Satan holds over people. His power to enslave in sin and the fear of death would be destroyed when Jesus was crucified and raised to life in victory by the power of God. It is the work of the Holy Spirit to assure believers—still engaged in combat with the fatally wounded enemy—that while the battles will continue for some time, the war has already been won. The final sentence has yet to be carried out, but the victory is certain because the prince of this world has already been judged. This is an often-overlooked work of the Spirit of God; but it was not missed by the disciples, who were in for their share of battles with the evil one in the days ahead. It serves as an anchor or kedge to any believers when they sense the evil one is prowling against them.

Jesus had already told Peter that Satan desired to sift him. Indeed, Peter would many times sense that he was in the crosshairs of the enemy. He would write in 1 Peter 5:8–9: "Be self-controlled and alert. Your enemy the devil prowls around like a roaring lion looking for someone to devour. Resist him, standing firm in the faith, because you know that your brothers throughout the world are undergoing the same kind of sufferings."

The warning is clear: Satan has been judged, but he is still dangerous. We can resist him, because while his fury has not been diminished, his power has been eliminated by the cross. A healthy understanding—fear balanced by knowledge of his judgment—enables us to be self-controlled and alert in response to the ever-present threat of the evil one.

Nellie Bazett was one of the first women missionaries in East Africa and the aunt of the famous anthropologist Louis Seymour Bazett Leakey (from whom I heard this story).[2] She sailed from England to Kenya with her sister Mary (Leakey's mother) with a leading from God to take the gospel inland to Uganda. The British administration would not let her travel across the African bush the eight hundred miles to Uganda. Mary returned to England where she married, later to return to Kenya with her husband, Harry.

Undaunted, Nellie hired her own porters and left under the cover of darkness for Uganda for what would be a trip of several months. Nellie arrived safely in Uganda and later reflected that her two most important pieces of equipment for the trip were her umbrella and her alarm clock. Nellie reasoned that her two biggest enemies across the bush would be the equatorial sun in the daytime and lions at night. She carried her umbrella during the day. At night she used her alarm clock to keep the lions away. The young missionary would set her alarm to go off every two hours during the night. She estimated that if a lion wanted to attack, it would require some time to stalk and approach the camp. When the alarm went off, the lion or lions, who might be stalking her and drawing close, would be scared back into the bush and have to begin their process of stalking all over again. That would give her two more hours to sleep. Nellie faithfully preached the gospel in Uganda for forty years. By sleeping in two-hour intervals in order to be safe, she was always self-controlled and alert.

Satan is still very dangerous, prowling for whom he may devour. Our healthy understanding of him as an enemy whom God has already judged is critical for our well-being. Although believing otherwise is easy, we live in a time of great spiritual warfare. The Holy Spirit assures our spirits that Satan's power is limited as a defeated enemy, and he helps us pray properly in a time of warfare.

Jesus also enumerated to his disciples yet another significant role of the Holy Spirit in the life of a believer, that of guide.

THE COMPASS CARRIER

"But when he, the Spirit of truth, comes, he will guide you into all truth" (John 16:13). These few verses of Scripture represent such a large conundrum. The riddle is easy enough to describe: if the Holy Spirit will guide us into all truth, why is there so much difference of opinion, of doctrine, and of teaching within Christendom?

Children killing children in the name of Christ in Uganda,[3] Catholic-Protestant violence in Ireland, and the rash of denominational splits in the North American church—all sides of these conflicts claim to have the right understanding of Scripture. We should recall the fear of one of the reformers that "Individual interpretation of the Bible allows each man to carve his own path to hell."[4]

The renewed publication of *The Jefferson Bible* in the last decade reminds us that it takes only a penknife to gut Scripture like a rainbow trout. Jefferson did just that and came up with a New Testament that had no miracles, no resurrection, no supernatural, no claims to deity—only the engaging teachings of Jesus, whom Jefferson regarded as the greatest moral teacher, eclipsing his philosophical patron saint Epicurus. Erik Reece, writing in the secular *Harper's* magazine, stated: "What's more, Jefferson's objection to the version of Christianity taught in American churches was precisely that it did put so much more emphasis on Jesus' life and, consequently, his sacrificial death. By excising the Resurrection and Jesus' claims to divinity from his private gospel, Jefferson portrayed an ordinary man with an extraordinary, though improbable, message. . . . Indeed, reading Jefferson's gospel one hundred years after its publication, it's hard not to become depressed, as did the Rich Young Ruler, about how nearly impossible Jesus' program would be to follow. . . . To read Jefferson's version . . . *is* to face a relentless demand that we be much better people—inside and out—than most of us are."[5]

Depressed indeed! It is not difficult to see the parallel between Jefferson's Bible and the attempts to accommodate the truth of God's Word to the postmodern culture, rather than to carefully exegete both and find the nexus. The German Lutheran church found ways to accommodate the age of national socialism while only Bonhoeffer and the Confessing Church remained faithful to the Word of God at great cost.[6] The North American church in the antebellum South made a similar accommodation to the slavery-based Southern culture and economy when it found justification for slavery and separation of the races in the Word of God.

The popularity of the "health and wealth gospel" preachers who obviously distort Scripture to fit their self-seeking theology is both puzzling and disturbing. Evangelicals continue to struggle with some teachings of the Catholic church that are clearly at odds with historical Protestant orthodoxy. We heard again at his funeral of the commitment Pope John Paul II had made to the adoration of Mary, a reminder that there remains a huge gulf between the two major streams of Christendom. Well-intentioned efforts to connect Protestant and Catholic understanding of the truth have been unsatisfactory at best.[7]

All of this has been within the mainstream of the church. Outside any semblance of orthodoxy, we regularly encounter new cults that claim they are the only true believers and they alone possess the "true truth" of God. We have seen believers (of some sort) follow Jim Jones, David Koresh, and Marshall Applewhite—and have been stunned at the distorted interpretations of the Bible they taught.

Betsy Childs put this discussion in a clear perspective when she wrote in "The King's Perspective" for *A Slice of Infinity*:

> You may have heard the famous story of the blind men and the elephant. In this story, a king leads several blind men to an elephant and asks them to describe it. The blind man feeling the elephant's leg says it is strong and straight like the trunk of a tree. The blind man holding the elephant's tail says it is long and flexible like a rope. The man feeling the elephant's side feels a great immovable wall, and the one touching the trunk says that it reminds him of a large snake.
>
> This story is usually told to point out that among the plurality of world religions, each contains only a portion of the total truth. It suggests that very disparate

ideas can be connected. People who tell this story want to make the point that if we could just see the total picture, we would forsake our disagreements and our exclusive claims and realize that we are all, so to speak, feeling the same elephant.

But if one leaves the story at that, its whole point is missed. Lesslie Newbigin, in his book *The Gospel in a Pluralist Society*, points out an important and often overlooked aspect of this story. He writes, "If the king were also blind there would be no story. The story is told by the king, and it is the immensely arrogant claim of one who sees the full truth which all the world's religions are only groping after."[8]

Our King told his disciples that he would give them the Holy Spirit to lead them into knowledge of all truth. Twenty centuries later we appear to be further from a consensus regarding the truth than ever before. The king is not blind; and he gave us the Spirit to lead us to the truth—but we have not all arrived at the same understanding of the truth.

The erroneous conclusion of some is that there is no truth. As Betsy Childs pointed out, that has been the conclusion of many religious observers and seekers. Since all the religions claim to be true, there must not be a true religion. That is as absurd as saying that because fifty students in my philosophy class all gave the wrong answer to the same question on the final exam, the question cannot have a right answer. It is an expression of the arrogance of our existential age to say that because I have not experienced the truth, it cannot exist.

More often than not, we have arrived at hundreds of different "truths" within the larger Christian movement because we simply do not read the Bible properly. Sometimes it is due to our deeply ingrained biases and traditions. Other times it is a matter of laziness or simple ignorance.[9] Often, not allowing the Spirit to lead us into all truth is the result of not knowing or applying some basic principles of how to read and understand different types of literature.[10] Walt Kaiser sounded an alarm in 1981 when he told us that there was a crisis in hermeneutics (the science of biblical interpretation): "The issue must be put bluntly: Is the meaning of a text to be defined solely in terms of the *verbal* meaning of that text as those words were used by the Scriptural author? Or should the meaning of a text be partly understood in terms of 'what it *now* means to me,' the reader and interpreter. There hangs one of the great dilemmas of our age. And there also hang the fortunes of the authority of Scripture."[11]

Kaiser's alarm rings again as loudly as Nellie Bazett's alarm clock: "There hangs one of the great dilemmas of our age. And there also hang the fortunes of the authority of Scripture." Every world religion makes its own truth claims, and certainly some truth can be found in each. Yet because Jesus said we are clean "because of the word I have spoken to you" (John 15:3), we have no eternal hope to offer anyone apart from the Word of God. Because he said, "I am the way and the truth and the life," we have no alternative to offer apart from the very words of the one who was the Word made flesh and dwelled among us. The challenge, indeed the dilemma, is to find those elusive, creative ways to engage the postmodern culture with the truth of God's Word and not compromise its integrity.

The frightening part is that what was a crisis of biblical authority and interpretation a generation ago is today no longer a crisis, at least for many, because there appears to have been a wholesale capitulation to the zeitgeist. Some in the emergent church are so eager to take Jesus to the postmodern culture that they have fully capitulated to and embraced postmodernism. Postmodernism argues that there is no metanarrative from which to construct a coherent worldview. Postmodernism finds no propositional truth and shuns anything that it judges as hierarchical truth. Richard Rorty wrote that "since there are many truths, there is no truth. Truth is what your friends will agree to."[12]

Others seem to have succumbed to what Ben Patterson in *The Wittenburg Door* once called the temptation of "turning stones into bread."[13] By that, he meant that we have a temptation to think that the Word of God will have relevance or meaning or power for our particular cultural setting only when we are able somehow—by our cleverness and insight—to transform these otherwise indigestible stones of the Bible into digestible bread others will find more appealing. It is hubris in any generation to believe that God needs us—with our exegetical skills, our philosophical wisdom, and our cultural savvy—to make the Word of God relevant to our particular generation.

The answer is not to subject the Bible to some type of alchemy. The answer is to allow the Holy Spirit to lead us into a deeper and richer understanding of the Word, where we find the answers to the question of postmodernism. That is what the Spirit has been tasked to do. He will lead us into all truth in any era if we are willing to engage all truth. It is not an easy process. Jesus recognized that his disciples could not handle all truth in a single dose. He had already given them more than they could handle and told them that the Spirit would lead them further as they were willing and able. This lifetime process of allowing the Spirit to lead us into all truth represents yet another anchor or kedge to take us through the difficult days of our lives as we walk with Christ by faith.

However, if "all Scripture is God-breathed" (2 Timothy 3:16), then some are not allowing the Spirit to lead them into all truth because the postmodern culture prefers one portion of Scripture or genre of Scripture and considers it superior to others. In truth, we need to guard against allowing our view of Scripture (or love for only certain portions of it) to be manipulated by the itching ears of a postmodern generation. If we fail to do so, we will soon witness publication of "The Postmodern Bible" (redacted for the postmodern era as Thomas Jefferson redacted the Bible for the Enlightenment), perhaps containing only narrative.

For our great trials and difficult times of tribulation, the Holy Spirit has been sent by the Father and the Son. He is God's comforting presence. He will also do among us what Jesus did by his physical presence—convict the world of sin, remind us of the righteousness of Christ, and remind us that the evil one has already been judged. He will also—if we will allow him—lead us into all the truth, a process that is not always comfortable. He is our comforter and our anchor who will pull us through.

OUR ANCHORAGE

The surprisingly popular *Deadliest Catch* has demonstrated with each episode that there is perhaps no more dangerous body of water than the North Pacific Ocean and the Bering Sea off the coast of the forty-ninth state. It is quite a contrast to Anchorage, the city on an inlet of calm waters and a safe harbor. On that evening when the disciples were facing great stress and trauma, Jesus told them about his plans for them to use their anchors to pull them through to an eternal anchorage: "In my Father's house are many rooms; if it were not so, I would have told you. I am going there to prepare a place for you. And if I go and prepare a place for you, I will come back and take you to be with me that you also may be where I am" (John 14:2–3).

To give peace to their troubled hearts, he promised to return and take them to be with him. We can only wonder what they understood about that at the moment he spoke it. Thomas expressed some uncertainty. Yet God's plan for his redeemed creation echoes through the Bible from Genesis to Revelation—that he will restore the order of Eden when he dwells with his people in unbroken fellowship: "My dwelling place will be with them; I will be their God, and they will be my people" (Ezekiel 37:27). "And I heard a loud voice from the throne saying, 'Now the dwelling of God is with men, and he will live with them. They will be his people, and God himself will be with them and be their God'" (Revelation 21:3).

The Bible contains hundreds of great and precious promises, but this, the ultimate bedrock promise for the child of God, serves as our anchorage—where we ultimately drop anchor. It is a promise that can take us through difficulties ranging from trivial to terminal. God has prepared an eternal home where he will dwell with us, again: "And I heard a loud voice from the throne saying, 'Now the dwelling of God is with men, and he will live with them. They will be his people, and God himself will be with them and be their God.'"[14] All the discussion of anchors is irrelevant unless we also know where the anchors are to be dropped. Collectively, the anchors Jesus provides serve to produce in us invaluable hope in a perfect storm.

The reflections of Victor Frankl on his fellow sufferers in the Nazi concentration camps bear witness to how essential to life itself is hope: "The prisoner who had lost faith in the future—his future—was doomed. With his loss of belief in the future, he also lost his spiritual hold; he let himself decline and became subject to mental and physical decay."[15] In our case as believers, hope ultimately comes from anchors set into the eternal. God might yet have a bright future for us in the aftermath of the storm, but it is knowing that our anchorage is set in the eternal that makes all hope real: "Therefore we do not lose heart. Though outwardly we are wasting away, yet inwardly we are being renewed day by day. For our light and momentary troubles are achieving for us an eternal glory that far outweighs them all. So we fix our eyes not on what is seen, but on what is unseen. For what is seen is temporary, but what is unseen is eternal" (2 Corinthians 4:16–18).

Paul took pains to confirm that the will of God is good and acceptable and perfect. The greatest test of our faith is summoned forth here. Trust in God. Trust also in Jesus who loves us, redeems us, and makes God known to us without distortion. Knowing God's character, trust in God's plan for your eternal future. Knowing God's promises—trusting God's plan for the eternal—enables us to trust God in the temporal. He will calm our troubled hearts as we pass through difficult times, and he will do so to the degree to which we trust in his control and grasp firmly our identity as his new creation in Christ: "Not only so, but we also rejoice in our sufferings, because we know that suffering produces perseverance; perseverance, character; and character, hope. And hope does not disappoint us, because God has poured out his love into our hearts by the Holy Spirit, whom he has given us" (Romans 5:3–5).

Our anchors are fixed in the eternal—where God reigns, where our citizenship is—so that we can say with the psalmist, "Find rest, O my soul, in God alone; my hope comes from him" (Psalm 62:5).

As a general rule we don't pay much attention to our breathing except when we have the wind knocked out of us or visit Colorado Springs and take the Pike's Peak Cog Railway to the top of Pike's Peak at 14,110 feet. Not so for me. I have been paying close attention to my breathing for several years now. When I am at home here at 6,600 feet, I have a continuous-flow oxygen concentrator; and when I travel, I drag along oxygen cylinders. Much of my life—schedule, limitations, expenses—revolves around what I used to not give much thought to, namely, breathing. I think constantly about the process of taking in a single breath. (I monitor my oxygen level every few minutes.) My pulmonologist recently sent me for some pulmonary rehabilitation therapy that included instruction on how to breathe differently to get more oxygen deeper into my lungs.[16] In class I learned how to breathe using my diaphragm rather than expanding my chest cavity, and I learned how to purse my lips as I exhaled to maintain a static pressure that maximizes the amount of time each breath is in my lungs. It requires concentration, paying attention to each breath—something that most people do without any conscious thought.

In addition, I now have a portable oxygen concentrator (POC) that I can take on airplanes. It also operates on a pulse system, giving me a measured bolus of oxygen when I inhale. My POC is something of a taskmaster, however. If I should fall asleep or doze even for a few moments on a flight (as I often do) and then stop breathing (as I often do because of sleep apnea), a nasty alarm sounds to get me breathing again. Breathing is serious business in my world, so thinking about breathing has been elevated to a new level. Breathing now is almost never subconscious but almost always a conscious process.

About the same time that I began my pulmonary rehabilitation, I began reading a book that surveys the spiritual disciples of A. B. Simpson, founder of the Christian and Missionary Alliance. Simpson's writings—the deeper life in the Spirit is the universal theme—can at times be difficult, penned in flowery one-hundred-year-old language befitting his era. Author Gary Keisling's initial chapter makes Simpson wonderfully accessible and begins with a focus on, of all things, how to breathe! Life in the Spirit—appropriating the indwelling transforming power of the Comforter, Confronter, and Compass—comes from giving continuous conscious attention to spiritually breathing in the Spirit and breathing out the self. Excerpts from a previously unpublished poem by Simpson, "Breathing Out and Breathing In" offer a compelling introduction to the pursuit and attainment of this deeper life in the Spirit:

> Jesus, breathe Thy Spirit on me
> Teach me how to breathe Thee in . . .
>
> I am breathing out my own life
> That I may be filled with Thine. . .
>
> Breathing out my sinful nature
> Thou hast borne it all for me.

Breathing in the cleansing fullness
Finding all my life in Thee.

I am breathing out my sorrow. . .
Breathing in Thy peace and rest.

I am breathing out my sickness. . .
I am breathing in Thy healing.

I am breathing out my longings. . .
I am breathing in Thy answers,
Stilling every doubt and fear.[17]

So we cultivate the life of the Spirit and know him as one who comforts, who searches our inner being, and guides us into deeper encounters with the truth. This is the fifth of our anchors and the one that enables us to kedge. He guides us. He shows us how and where to set our other anchors. He gives us strength. He gives us courage and hope in the perfect storm.

PART III
ADMONITIONS

9

ADMONITION 1:
TRUST

(THE ANTIDOTE FOR A TROUBLED HEART)

DO NOT LET YOUR HEARTS BE TROUBLED. TRUST IN
GOD; TRUST ALSO IN ME.

"Trust in God; trust also in me." Unpacking the seven words of this exhortation is no small challenge, but it is vital that we do so because it represents another critical anchor. It is the antidote for a troubled heart.

Pastor John Piper was diagnosed in late 2005 with prostate cancer. In a letter to his congregation, he wrote:

> The news of cancer has a wonderfully blasting effect on both [the sin of self-reliance and the stupor of the world]. I thank God for that. The times with Christ in these days have been unusually sweet.
>
> For example, is there anything greater to hear and believe in the bottom of your heart than this: "God has not destined us for wrath, but to obtain salvation through our Lord Jesus Christ, who died for us so that

whether we are awake or asleep we might live with him" (1 Thessalonians 5:9–10)?[1]

All of us aspire to such faith, assurance, and peace at those times when our own world seems to be crumbling into pieces. We would all like to stare down a crisis in our lives with the same sort of confidence in God. While our clear sense of identity as a child of God is a priceless, stable foundation, a confidence born of a strong sense of our own identity is vital. It is an anchor. But there is more. We must develop a confidence born also of a solid understanding of the identity of the one into whose hands we have entrusted our lives and our eternal destiny. A kedge, recall, is a worthwhile tool for navigating life, but the kedge needs to be anchored in the right place to be of value. So while our sense of identity as children of God is vitally important, of equal or greater importance is our solid understanding of the identity and character of our heavenly Father. Jesus' exhortation to not be troubled is leveraged by our trust in God the Father and trust in Christ.

TWO SIDES OF THE SAME DENARIUS

Trust, it seems, has both active and passive elements. We exercise our faith when we ask God for what we need (or want). It is, or should be, a daily process, according to the Lord's Prayer. We sign mortgages on our homes, trusting that God will supply our needs and we will be able to pay the mortgage. We plant churches, trusting that God will draw people to himself and that the work of the kingdom will be advanced. Missionaries depart for the far corners of the globe, trusting that God will provide, protect, and prosper the work of their hands. Prayer itself is an act of trust as we invest time and energy in asking God for the many things on our hearts or lists, believing that God does reward those who diligently seek him. That is why Jesus promised: "If you remain in me and my words remain in you, ask whatever you wish, and it will be given you" (John 15:7).

It is a remarkable and often misunderstood promise that is easily exploited by the teachers of false gospels. The promise is true but tempered by the teaching that God answers all things in accordance with his will. Those who live in Christ and in whom his word lives will ask according to God's will and find those requests fulfilled. Prayer is an expression of faith, just as is every act of obedience and every temptation resisted.

The other side of the denarius (a Roman coin) is that trust is also passive. Job, as much as anyone, demonstrated this passive aspect of trust when he said that no matter what God allowed to come his way, he would continue to trust God. Four pithy statements from the account in Job summarize the reality of passive trust:

- "The LORD gave and the LORD has taken away; may the name of the LORD be praised" (1:21).
- "Shall we accept good from God, and not trouble?" (2:10).
- "Though he slay me, yet will I hope in him" (13:15).
- "I know that my Redeemer lives, and that in the end he will stand upon the earth. And after my skin has been destroyed, yet in my flesh I will see God (19:25–26).

In our times of crisis, we pray fervently—perhaps even debating with God as Job did—that God might alter the circumstances, all the while remembering that prayer is an act of trust. But when God's will reveals that we must pass through the crisis, we learn to surrender our will as an act of trust as well. Trust involves acceptance and an embrace of God's will. It involves surrender to God's will. Jesus prayed that he might not have to drink the cup, but then he surrendered to the will of God.

THE NATURE OF OUR ANXIETIES

Anxiety is psychological pain that tells us something is wrong or could be wrong in the immediate future. It may be an uneasiness of unknown origin, or it might be rooted in a specific and identifiable set of circumstances. Although we rightly question much of what Paul Tillich wrote, his suggestion that there are three forms or categories of anxiety seems correct:

- anxiety related to fate and death
- anxiety related to emptiness and meaninglessness
- anxiety related to guilt and condemnation[2]

This supports the conclusion of others that these are related to our being (ontological anxieties) rather than anxieties linked to some specific event.[3] From a Christian perspective these three expressions of anxiety overlap and are at the heart of our brokenness caused by sin and the fall. The writer of Hebrews brings together so many truths in two verses: "Since the children have flesh and blood, he too shared in their humanity so that by his death he might destroy him who holds the power of death—that is, the devil—and free those who all their lives were held in slavery by their fear of death" (Hebrews 2:14–15).

The foundational anxiety, always playing in the background of our lives, is the fear of death. Along with that, the fear of condemnation is with us if we have never experienced the grace of God. And for many, the anxiety of meaninglessness exists because God has "set eternity in the hearts of men" (Ecclesiastes 3:11), resulting in dissonance between the temporal, material life and the prospect of eternal life.

Anxiety abounded around the table as Jesus spoke with the Eleven in the upper room. At that moment Jesus well might have been experiencing some anxiety himself. Within perhaps an hour in the garden of Gethsemane, he would experience not only anxiety but the ravages of a deeply troubled spirit that struggled with the cup he had to drink. Jesus knew that all things had been placed under his authority, that he had come from God, and that he was returning to God. His identity and his complete knowledge of what was to transpire were the kedges that would pull him through this darkest hour of the soul. Even as he was experiencing anxiety and would soon pass through despair, he was anchored by his knowledge of who he was, his knowledge that all things were under his authority by God's design, and that he was drinking this cup in obedience to his Father—obedience practiced and perfected in suffering.

Being on the threshold of his own crisis with its understandable assault on the psyche, Jesus sought to give relief to his inner circle of followers. Their anxiety was somewhat different from his. His was the anxiety of knowing in detail the horrible ordeal that was unfolding. Theirs was the anxiety of not knowing. His anxiety included his concern for them. Their anxiety was primarily rooted in concern for themselves. We could debate which is the greater: the anxiety of not knowing what will happen or the anxiety of knowing. Most of us don't know what will happen, and our anxiety is rooted in not knowing.

THE ONE ANTIDOTE FOR ANXIETY

The antidote for anxiety that Jesus prescribed for the disciples was simple enough: "You trust in God; trust also in me." We might well begin with the question, Since Jesus is God, what is the difference in trusting in God (the Father) and trusting in God (the Son)? We must first recognize the obvious: we have a different perspective than the disciples did at that moment. Jesus was physically still with them, although only for a few more hours, and they were just beginning to understand the implications of Jesus' deity. They may have not pondered the mystery of the triune God. Jesus, they observed, was a person who claimed and demonstrated his deity, but they saw him often praying to the Father. They heard him speak of the Father. They saw his submission to the Father. The distinction between the Father and the Son was, at least for that brief season of history, something they seem to have been able to comprehend.

Of course, Jesus would begin to confound them a few moments

later as he interacted with Phillip: "Philip said, 'Lord, show us the Father and that will be enough for us.' Jesus answered: 'Don't you know me, Philip, even after I have been among you such a long time? Anyone who has seen me has seen the Father. How can you say, "Show us the Father"? Don't you believe that I am in the Father, and that the Father is in me? The words I say to you are not just my own. Rather, it is the Father, living in me, who is doing his work'" (John 14:8–10).

We can well understand that the disciples were having difficulty comprehending at this point. They perceived that Jesus and the Father are not the same person, and they understood, "Trust in God, trust also in me." Only moments later Jesus presented an apparent contradiction—to see Jesus is to see the Father because they are one. That apparent contradiction we have come to know as the mystery of the Trinity, and we ought not to be surprised if we cannot comprehend it. We are finite and the Trinity is an infinite reality.

The human psyche is complex and nearly incomprehensible. We are body, spirit, will, intellect, and emotions (together—according to some—will, intellect, and emotions make up the soul). And how all of those aspects of a singular person interact is nearly impossible to diagram or trace or measure. Yet we are one person. How much more complex and beyond our finite ability to understand is the psyche of the eternal one-in-three? If we could understand God in three persons, then he would not be God. Our difficulty, wrote the late Ken Kantzer, is that while God is one and God is three, he is one in a different way than he is three: "We are not saying something foolish or contradictory—that God is both three and one in the same sense at the same time. We are simply saying that God's inner make up is different from ours. In one of His aspects He is three. In quite a different aspect He is one."[4] We need only look to quantum physics for an example. Light, when measured as a wave, has velocity (186,000 miles per second) but no mass. However, if we measure the same light as a particle, it has mass but ceases to have velocity. So from one perspective God is one; at the same time but from a different perspective, God is three.

A number of years ago I read a story in *Reader's Digest* that illustrates our problem with the triune nature of God. A man came home one evening and discovered that an area rug from his living room had been wadded up and stuffed into his kitchen sink. He was bewildered how this could have happened in his locked apartment and attempted to extricate the carpet from the sink. He pulled at it, but to no avail. He went to call for help, and as he was waiting for the elevator, he related his strange tale to his neighbor. Cracking up, the neighbor took him to his apartment and showed him three exhausted maintenance workers frantically pulling on a plumber's snake in the kitchen sink. As they compared notes, they soon realized what had happened. From the neighbor's sink the snake had made a wrong turn in the plumbing tree of the apartment complex and emerged from the sink in the next apartment. The snake then extended into the living room, where it snagged the area rug. When the plumber sought to retrieve the snake, he could not because the hooked area rug could not fit through the plumbing tree. So it is with us. We can ask questions about the triune God, but most of the time what we snag in the way of answers are pieces of the infinite that will not fit through the finite pipeline of our own minds. The finite cannot process the infinite, and no apologies are needed.

We reveal how different our perspectives are by the patterns of prayer. Many Christians pray to Jesus. They seek to spend time with Christ in their devotional lives. Others (and I think rightly) have concluded that the teaching of Scripture is that we ought to pray to the Father, in the Spirit, and in the name of Jesus. They tend to speak of their walk with God. There is little question that God in three persons is a challenge to our finite psyches, even as revealed by our conceptualization of prayer. The challenge of understanding the

Godhead is complicated further by the common distortions we have about God.

OUR FOUR GOD DISTORTIONS

As a pastor for nearly three decades, I have encountered people with no faith or understanding of God. I have also encountered a number of people with mushy faith in God. I never have quite been able to determine the exact meaning of an expression I have heard many times, "I believe in God and stuff." "God and stuff" is a curious aphorism. Sadly, many who consider themselves people of faith have a faith no more refined or focused than "God and stuff." As widespread as this fuzzy concept of God is, it is usually based on ignorance, something that can be easily addressed when there is a willing or open mind and heart.

More difficult to address are the distorted ideas people have about God, especially the distorted views of God held by people who should know better. Perhaps the best-known and most obvious God distortions are summarized in John Koster's insightful book, *The Atheist Syndrome*. In this seminal volume Koster detailed the lives of some of the best-known and perhaps infamous atheists of the past one hundred years, men who significantly shaped twentieth-century culture. The common thread among them is that all were raised in homes where fathers were cold, distant, judgmental, harsh, or even cruel to their sons. All were alleged to be godly men or at least God fearers, but the lifetime impact on their children was profound and tragic. Many of their children grew to hate God as they projected on to a heavenly Father their resentment toward their earthly fathers. We might even conclude that these infamous atheists were actually God haters rather than true atheists. The damage in their lives is palpable. They all were depressed and ultimately sickly much of their adult lives. Charles Darwin, Thomas Huxley, Friedrich Nietzsche, Sigmund Freud, Robert Ingersoll, and Clarence Darrow—the renowned atheists of their generations—generally lived the second half of their lives with deep depression and debilitating physical ailments. Although each professed strict philosophical atheism, there appeared to Koster to be a great deal of hostility toward the allegedly nonexistent God.[5] A pattern of a cruel or distant father that leads to a severe God distortion that leads to hatred of God is clearly demonstrated. As I teach philosophy at a secular college, I continue to be saddened by my students' papers that profess atheism but between the lines reveal an enormous hostility toward this God who "does not exist." The extent of a God distortion can be far reaching indeed.

A few years ago when most churches still had choirs, ours had a choir director of fine musical ability but very unusual tastes. Each week I told her themes for worship services so that she would find compatible choral selections; and for two years of her ministry she regularly selected anthems from eighteenth- and nineteenth-century Russian composers with names I neither knew nor could pronounce. After many months—and some fine choral performances, I will admit—it became clear that we did not see eye to eye regarding choral music. Sometime after this music director stepped down, my administrative assistant compiled a list of all her choir selections during her tenure. The average date for the pieces was the 1790s, and there was a commonality about each—all the songs were about or addressed to a transcendent God who was distant, unreachable, and even fearful (which he can be). There were few if any references to Jesus. Most were focused on God the Father. Not one selection came close to speaking about the love of God or the immanence of God; the selections always focused on his greatness, grandeur, and awesomeness instead. He was never portrayed in the music as "close to the brokenhearted" or near to us in any way. This was not just a matter of musical taste—this was a theological matter, as we had significant differences in how we comprehended God. She envisioned a distant, transcendent, almost impersonal God. I was seeking to tell people from the pulpit about a loving God who was also present with us in the worship service. It prompted a great deal of reflection on my part as to the different distortions we may have concerning God. This was not resentment and hatred of God like the atheists mentioned, but this was a distortion nonetheless and a distortion that impaired a follower of Jesus Christ from glorifying God by enjoying him forever.

Around this same time, I discovered the writings of Dr. Frank Lake, a thoroughly orthodox British psychologist. In *Clinical Theology*[6]—not psychology—Lake posited that each of us has, to a greater or lesser degree, a God distortion. There are, according to Lake, four major personality types, and each has its own unique God distortion. And while no model is perfect, Lake's model appears to have a strong resemblance to reality. Lake described each one in great depth in his unabridged volume of some nine hundred pages. The abridged version, a more manageable three hundred pages, provides very adequate summaries. My brief synopsis will hardly do justice to Lake's in-depth analysis. And while I am aware that there are softer consumer-oriented expressions of "personality types" involving otters and retrievers and the like, I want to be faithful to the author.

DEPRESSIVE PERSONALITY TYPE

I start with the depressive personality type because I find myself to be afflicted with this distortion to a greater or lesser degree at various times. The depressive person manifests sadness, anger, and at times a strong sense of guilt. Jeff VanVonderen in *Tired of Trying to Measure Up*[7] describes how many depressive people were raised in homes where love was conditional and they had to perform at certain levels to feel loved and approved. Depressive people project onto God much of the image of their earthly parents and conclude that God is angry, judging, and eager to punish his children. They struggle to appropriate the love and unconditional acceptance of God that is found in Jesus Christ, who said, "You are already clean because of the word I have spoken to you" (John 15:3). Since love at home in the nuclear family had to be earned, a parallel God distortion evolves. God's love is perceived as conditional and must be worked for. Depressive people tend to gravitate to legalism in their relationship with God in hope that if they can behave in a more Christlike manner, or practice better sin management, or serve God in a more productive way, God will love them more.

Lake went on to suggest that two common factors stifle the depressive person's inflow of acceptance: lust and anger. Depressive people are in a fix regarding anger. They are often angry at God because of their frustration with being on a treadmill as they try to gain more of God's favor. But they cannot process that anger because they also are very nervous about being angry at God. They have concluded that they cannot tell God how angry they are because God would punish them for this feeling by withholding acceptance and blessing. To a great degree the inability to process this anger toward God causes depression and solidifies the depressive personality type. For the depressive person, false guilt becomes a constant battle and a source of continued anxiety about acceptance.

Lust is seriously damaging to our relationship with God because it blocks our ability and desire to hear from God. It becomes a spiritual catch-22. Depressive people need to hear repeatedly (daily, even hourly) the assurance of God's love. However, lust keeps them from hearing from God and results in an even greater distance from the source of acceptance and nurture that they need.

According to Lake, this sense of isolation from God often leads to greater struggles with lust because fantasy is more a sign of loneliness than it is of badness. Like many men who have struggled with lust, I testify that these descriptions of behavior patterns are accurate. Jonah is an example of a biblical personality who might well have had a depressive personality type and the corresponding God distortion. His depressive tendencies are apparent in their expressed desire

NAVIGATING YOUR PERFECT STORM

for his life to end because he could not find rest in the perfect love of God.

I'll leave to you the rereading of the full account of this prophet who served God in extraordinary ways in spite of his depressive personality. But don't miss the expressions of his depressive personality: "But Jonah was greatly displeased and became angry. He prayed to the LORD, 'O LORD, is this not what I said when I was still at home? That is why I was so quick to flee to Tarshish. I knew that you are a gracious and compassionate God, slow to anger and abounding in love, a God who relents from sending calamity. Now, O LORD, take away my life, for it is better for me to die than to live'" (Jonah 4:1–3).

Yet God was repeatedly patient and gracious with Jonah, whom he instructed about his character.

God was also patient and nurturing with Elijah, another depressive:

> He came to a broom tree, sat down under it and prayed that he might die. "I have had enough, LORD," he said. "Take my life; I am no better than my ancestors." Then he lay down under the tree and fell asleep.
>
> All at once an angel touched him and said, "Get up and eat." He looked around, and there by his head was a cake of bread baked over hot coals, and a jar of water. He ate and drank and then lay down again.
>
> The angel of the LORD came back a second time and touched him and said, "Get up and eat, for the journey is too much for you." So he got up and ate and drank. Strengthened by that food, he traveled forty days and forty nights until he reached Horeb, the mountain of God (1 Kings 19:4–8).

It would appear that Elijah was not unlike us, for he might well have shared more than one personality type. There is some evidence of a paranoid personality, for he told God upon his arrival at Mount Horeb that he was the only follower of God left in all of Israel (v. 10), which was not true.

HYSTERIC PERSONALITY TYPE

The hysteric personality type is marked not by sadness but by anxiety. This personality type, summarized Lake, is marked by fear of abandonment and fear of being alone. There is a tendency to cling in relationships out of fear of letting go. The fear of abandonment may have had its seeds planted early in life by an unfulfilled need for a connection with a parent at a critical time. Projected onto God, this unfulfilled need results in a distorted view of a God who is abandoning and cannot be trusted to be there for us when we need him.

With the profusion of cellular technology, many in the Gen-X and millennial generation remain electronically connected to their network of peers every waking moment. If they are not online via a laptop, they are connected through their cell phones—calling, text messaging, sending pictures. Sending an "I'm going to the mall for an hour" to every person on their network is an expression of anxiety and a plea for others not to sign off. This anxiety is the frequent companion of the person who is a hysteric.

Mary, who was quite different from her eager-to-please sister Martha, might well have been a hysteric. We find her in the Gospels clinging to the feet of Jesus—first at the dinner at their home just a few days before Passover and later just after the resurrection, when she encountered Jesus in the garden. Jesus praised her for choosing to be at his feet, but we can assume that she had her own psychological need to be there and could not be budged by all of Martha's appeals for help. Perhaps Mary was clinging because she had separation anxiety rooted in her fear that Jesus would leave again.

Lake's perspective on the hysteric personality is that the hysteric always needs to be with someone. For the hysteric, waiting time is dying time, and separation and time alone are extremely painful. In addition, there is a tendency toward being histrionic or melodramatic—even small events get blown out of proportion. For hysterics, their relationships frequently are marked by some patterns that are the result of this need. The hysteric person needs to learn how to be alone and how to be quiet and listen.

SCHIZOID PERSONALITY TYPE

A very different personality is the schizoid personality type. Clearly distinguished from the commonly held ideas of schizophrenia as a "split personality," the schizoid personality is marked by a fear of intimacy, of getting too close in relationships. The pressure to commit causes great anxiety and irritability. There is a resulting pattern of detachment and introversion. This may result from trauma in early life that causes the goodness and even the existence of God to come into question.

What evolves from this fear is a distortion of God as capricious or faceless. I saw this distortion in my choir director who viewed God as distant and transcendent; God cannot be known intimately but only conceptually. God is known by his attributes of sovereignty, omnipotence, holiness, and otherness. It is barely possible for the schizoid person to know God intimately as a loving and personal God. This individual has trouble trusting when it requires taking a step closer.

Thomas, better known as Doubting Thomas, possessed a strong left-brain orientation. His trouble trusting and fear of commitment might have been rooted in this personality type, but we know too little about him to be certain. Job, on the other hand, serves as a good example of the schizoid type of personality. Job thought God distant and capricious. Job despaired but was unwilling to face this head on. "What I feared has come upon me . . . I have no rest, but only turmoil" (Job 3:25–26). He had a great sense of alienation from God and even from his friends who came to be with him. They said nothing for seven days, and Job was content in this isolation. Job affirmed his innocence to his friends and to God and cut himself off from any consolation that might come from his friends or God. As his friends unloaded guilt and recrimination on him through a cycle of speeches, Job became even more alienated, isolated, and argumentative. He ultimately expressed his desire to die, something he preferred to being healed. As he sensed that even more suffering might come at the hand of God, his fear of "the other shoe falling" caused him to recede from God even further. In the midst of his perfect storm, Job perceived a faceless God: "When he passes me, I cannot see him; when he goes by, I cannot perceive him" (Job 9:11). He believed God to be not loving but capricious: "He would crush me with a storm and multiply my wounds for no reason" (Job 9:17).

Scorn is inseparable from the schizoid: "How then can I dispute with him? How can I find words to argue with him? Though I were innocent, I could not answer him; I could only plead with my Judge for mercy. Even if I summoned him and he responded, I do not believe he would give me a hearing" (Job 9:14–16).

Clearly, few of us have suffered as much as Job, but we all need to learn from Job and his darkest days. Job asked, "How can a mortal be righteous before God?" (Job 9:1). And while his friends could never answer that question properly,[8] Job answered that critical question himself—an answer with significant prophetic overtones: "If only there were someone to arbitrate between us, to lay his hand upon us both, someone to remove God's rod from me, so that his terror would frighten me no more. Then I would speak up without fear of him, but as it now stands with me, I cannot" (Job 9:33–35).

We know now who it is that Job longed for, a mediator between God and man who would remove God's punishment, who would so clearly demonstrate the love of God that we would never have reason to doubt his loving character. Yet at the time, Job could not see past his own suffering.

PARANOID PERSONALITY TYPE

The last of the personality types is the paranoid personality type: touchy, defensive, wary of critics, argumentative, and without gracious humor. While all of us can have feelings of paranoia at those times when people or problems confront us, the paranoid personality type is marked by a continual life of recurring suspicion and doubt. People with paranoid personalities live with the fear that what they hold as the foundation of security in life will be taken away. According to Frank Lake, the paranoid personality type is the result not of a traumatic event or broken relationships but is normally the result of a lack of spiritual nurture. The result is a perception of God as absconding, self-serving, or even destructive.

John the Baptist may well have had a paranoid personality, especially at the time he was imprisoned by Herod. While he was active in his preaching ministry, it was not difficult for John to say of Jesus, "He must become greater; I must become less" (John 3:30). Later when John's own ministry as the herald of the coming Messiah had been effectively completed and John had been imprisoned by Herod, the distortion become more evident. Cut off not only from public ministry, confined in prison, and without the nurture he needed, John was also cut off from an ongoing relationship with his cousin Jesus:

> John's disciples told him about all these things. Calling two of them, he sent them to the Lord to ask, "Are you the one who was to come, or should we expect someone else?"
>
> When the men came to Jesus, they said, "John the Baptist sent us to you to ask, 'Are you the one who was to come, or should we expect someone else?'"
>
> At that very time Jesus cured many who had diseases, sicknesses and evil spirits, and gave sight to many who were blind. So he replied to the messengers, "Go

back and report to John what you have seen and heard:
The blind receive sight, the lame walk, those who have
leprosy are cured, the deaf hear, the dead are raised,
and the good news is preached to the poor. Blessed
is the man who does not fall away on account of me"
(Luke 7:18–23).

Yet Jesus said of cousin John that "among those born of women
there is no one greater than John; yet the one who is least in the
kingdom of God is greater than he" (Luke 7:28). I find that encour-
aging. God knows our psychological realities. Jesus sent a message to
encourage John.

IMPLICATIONS OF OUR
FOUR GOD DISTORTIONS

These brief descriptions of personality types and their corresponding God distortions are simplistic. This short exposition is not
designed to be definitive but illustrative, to help us think about the
reality that we all have at least one God distortion. The chart that follows identifies four biblical characters who demonstrate some char-
acteristics of these personality types and who might help us think
through our own God distortions.

Because everyone has a God distortion to a greater or lesser degree, all of us need to consider the implications of Jesus' earlier statement: "Trust in God; trust also in me." The first implication, then, is
that "trust in God" means very different things to different people—
even very different things among Christians.

Some believers see God as stern, angry, abandoning, absconding, capricious, or self-serving, depending on their own particular
distortion. We may agree on the list of God's attributes as compiled
by theologians, but we emphasize different aspects of God's character
according to our own bent. For seventeenth-century Russian composers and those who esteem their choral works, God is transcendent

Bible Character	Elijah	Mary	Job	John the Baptist
Personality Type	Depressive	Hysteric	Schizoid	Paranoid
Typical Distortion: "God is. . ."	Angry Eager to punish	Rejecting Abandoning	Faceless Capricious	Self-serving Destructive
Major Fear	Fear of not being loved	Fear of being alone	Fear of intimacy	Fear of loss of security
Typical Traits	Sad Lustful Angry at God	Anxious Clingy Histrionic	Strongly left-brained Introverted Detached	Fearful Defensive Suspicious
Resistance to grace	Legalistic	Impulsive	Distrusting	Defensive
Helpful Scriptures	Ps. 42 & 43 Galatians	Heb. 4:6–11 Lk. 10:41–42	Mt. 11:4–6 Ps. 88 & 73 Job	1 Peter 4:13–16

and distant. For those who prefer a more contemporary expression of worship, God is imminent, an awesome presence with his children. But some of us who believe in a good God still have trouble trusting him.

The second implication is that to trust in God truly, we need to begin by trusting in Jesus. This does not mean that God cannot be known apart from Christ, for certainly he was known to Abraham and all who, like Abraham, believed God and found it was counted as righteousness. God has been about the business of revealing himself since creation. Paul told the Romans: "For since the creation of the world God's invisible qualities—his eternal power and divine nature—have been clearly seen, being understood from what has been made, so that men are without excuse. For although they knew God, they neither glorified him as God nor gave thanks to him" (1:20–21).

But neither creation nor the Old Testament is the pinnacle of God's revelation. The complete revelation of God concerning his character, his will, and his love is found in the person of Jesus. "In the past God spoke to our forefathers through the prophets at many times and in various ways, but in these last days he has spoken to us by his Son, whom he appointed heir of all things, and through whom he made the universe. The Son is the radiance of God's glory and the exact representation of his being, sustaining all things by his powerful word" (Hebrews 1:1–3).

If I might paraphrase and expand on Jesus' words, he was saying something like this to his disciples: "You believe in God whom you know imperfectly, now believe and find a complete knowledge of God through me." When Phillip challenged Jesus to "show us the Father," Jesus told him that "anyone who has seen me has seen the Father," because the Father was living in Jesus (John 14:9–10).

Trusting in God means trusting in Jesus, and this is the foundation for the exclusive statement Jesus made to his disciples: "I am the way the truth and the life. No one comes to the Father except by me" (John 14:6). Because God sent his Son into the world to make known the Father and to provide for our salvation, then it is unthinkable that God would have provided another way or, as some suggest, many other ways to know him. The exclusive truth claim of the Christian faith is anchored here. If Jesus came as the culmination of God's revelation in history, then it is impossible to have a complete and accurate knowledge of God apart from Jesus. Handicapped as we are with our various God distortions, our knowledge of God is woefully inadequate or erroneous. This is why Paul said, "Although they *knew God*, they neither glorified him as God nor gave thanks to him" (Romans 1:21, emphasis added). The knowledge of God by the

NAVIGATING YOUR PERFECT STORM

natural man is incomplete and distorted by sin and its brokenness—
all of which results in our catalog of God distortions.

Further, trusting God by trusting Jesus is the key to dealing with
our God distortions. The distorted views that God is stern, angry,
abandoning, absconding, capricious, or self-serving are corrected
and perfected at the cross of Jesus Christ. There the perfect redemp-
tive and restorative love of God was poured out and the possibility of a warm, intimate fellowship with Christ was established. It is
through Jesus that we come to know God, not the other way around.
(Which raises the curious question of apologetics, Do we begin with
the existence of God and then move toward Christ, or the other way
around?)

It is a long and circuitous way from the initial questions of this
chapter to this conclusion, but the answer to our troubled hearts is
a warm, personal, intimate faith walk with our Savior, who loved us
and gave himself for us. Our hearts will not be troubled when we
believe in God and believe also in him. It is in knowing Jesus in vital
communion that our anxieties—such a large part of our God distortions—are revealed, redressed, and removed. As we walk by faith in
relationship with Jesus, not with a fuzzy "God and stuff" deity, we
come to understand his merciful character and his gracious plan for
those he has purchased and made adopted children of God.

Bill Leslie had reached a point of burnout after years of pastoral ministry at LaSalle Street Church in the inner city of Chicago.
The church was not very large—a few hundred—but carried out
dozens of ministries to the community and employed more than a
hundred people. Bill had been mugged, shot, and regularly threatened by drug dealers—all part of ministry in the city. He told me
years later when we became acquainted that he felt like the village
pump—everyone came, pumped what they wanted from him, and
then took off. He began to withdraw, unplugged the phone, and
curled into a ball emotionally and psychologically. His physician sent
him for counseling, and he received a surprise when he discovered

his counselor to be a Roman Catholic nun. After he had unpacked his story for her, he received a bigger surprise. She told him, "Bill, what you really need is a warm, loving, personal relationship with Jesus Christ." Bill told me he thought, *Wait! I'm the evangelical. I'm supposed to tell her that!*

I never had a chance to talk to him about how his view of God—a God distortion—had inhibited his relationship with Christ or how the counseling brought him to the obvious new place he was when I met him near the end of his journey.[9]

Our antidote for anxiety in our difficulties is rooted in our trust in the promises of Jesus. That is not an expression of mere fideism or "faith in faith." We must also believe what Jeremiah recorded as God's promise: "I know the plans I have for you, plans to prosper you and not to harm you, plans to give you hope and a future" (Jeremiah 29:11).

Overcoming Obstacles to Prayer

Learning how to pray may very well require overcoming the inertia not only of the common problems I mentioned above (not believing it makes any difference, self-sufficiency, and guilt), but also our individual God distortions. Not only does each of the four personality types have a God distortion, but each of those God distortions impacts the owner's prayer life. And for each a specific nurture of the spirit is needed to overcome that distortion.

For the depressive personality type, the emphasis must be on the grace and unconditional love of God. Depressive believers will have a tendency to turn away from what they perceive to be the legalism of a strictly disciplined devotional life that requires a pattern of Bible reading and journaling and the like. They would benefit from a focus on Galatians and here, Psalm 42:

> As the deer pants for streams of water, so my soul
> pants for you, O God.

My soul thirsts for God, for the living God. When
can I go and meet with God?
My tears have been my food day and night,
while men say to me all day long, "Where is your
God?"
These things I remember as I pour out my soul:
how I used to go with the multitude, leading the
procession to the house of God,
with shouts of joy and thanksgiving among the festive
throng.
Why are you downcast, O my soul? Why so disturbed
within me?
Put your hope in God, for I will yet praise him, my
Savior and my God.
My soul is downcast within me; therefore I will
remember you
from the land of the Jordan, the heights of
Hermon—from Mount Mizar.
Deep calls to deep in the roar of your waterfalls;
all your waves and breakers have swept over me.
By day the LORD directs his love, at night his song is
with me—a prayer to the God of my life. . . .
. . . Why are you downcast, O my soul? Why so
disturbed within me?
Put your hope in God, for I will yet praise him, my
Savior and my God.

Some people need to be reminded regularly, even constantly, of
God's unconditional love. He will not love us more if we have a more
regular quiet time. Our devotional lives are not for his benefit and
therefore are not a source of merit in God's sight. The nurture of a
devotional life is a benefit for us, however, and Hebrews 4 seems a
critical message in this regard:

There remains, then, a Sabbath-rest for the people of God; for anyone who enters God's rest also rests from his own work, just as God did from his. Let us, therefore, make every effort to enter that rest, so that no one will fall by following their example of disobedience.

For the word of God is living and active. Sharper than any double-edged sword, it penetrates even to dividing soul and spirit, joints and marrow; it judges the thoughts and attitudes of the heart. Nothing in all creation is hidden from God's sight. Everything is uncovered and laid bare before the eyes of him to whom we must give account.

Therefore, since we have a great high priest who has gone through the heavens, Jesus the Son of God, let us hold firmly to the faith we profess. For we do not have a high priest who is unable to sympathize with our weaknesses, but we have one who has been tempted in every way, just as we are—yet was without sin. Let us then approach the throne of grace with confidence, so that we may receive mercy and find grace to help us in our time of need.

He is always there and there for us. No appointment necessary.

Still others need to learn to trust. The schizoid personality type would benefit from learning to trust at a significant new level. Matthew 11:4–6 is an encouragement not to fall away. And Psalm 88 might serve as a connection point with God for the one who is afraid of drawing too close:

O Lord, the God who saves me, day and night I cry
   out before you.
May my prayer come before you; turn your ear to my cry.
For my soul is full of trouble and my life draws near
   the grave.

I am counted among those who go down to the pit; I
am like a man without strength.

I am set apart with the dead, like the slain who lie in
the grave,

whom you remember no more, who are cut off from
your care.

You have put me in the lowest pit, in the darkest depths.

Your wrath lies heavily upon me; you have
overwhelmed me with all your waves. *Selah*

You have taken from me my closest friends and have
made me repulsive to them.

I am confined and cannot escape; my eyes are dim
with grief.

I call to you, O LORD, every day; I spread out my
hands to you.

Do you show your wonders to the dead? Do those
who are dead rise up and praise you? *Selah*

Is your love declared in the grave, your faithfulness in
Destruction?

Are your wonders known in the place of darkness, or
your righteous deeds in the land of oblivion?

But I cry to you for help, O LORD; in the morning
my prayer comes before you.

Why, O LORD, do you reject me and hide your face
from me?

From my youth I have been afflicted and close to
death; I have suffered your terrors and am in
despair.

Your wrath has swept over me; your terrors have
destroyed me.

All day long they surround me like a flood; they have
completely engulfed me.

> You have taken my companions and loved ones from
> me; the darkness is my closest friend.

The paranoid personality type needs to know that difficulty in life is not the result of God's rejection. We live in a sinful world, and difficulties are woven into the fabric of every life. Such believers can be nurtured by the reinforcement of Romans 8 that nothing can separate us from the love of God, but that doesn't mean that we will be separated from difficulties in life. It may be necessary to reinforce the truths of Hebrews 12:5–11:

> My son, do not make light of the Lord's discipline,
> and do not lose heart when he rebukes you,
> because the Lord disciplines those he loves, and he
> punishes everyone he accepts as a son.
>
> Endure hardship as discipline; God is treating you as sons. For what son is not disciplined by his father? If you are not disciplined (and everyone undergoes discipline), then you are illegitimate children and not true sons. Moreover, we have all had human fathers who disciplined us and we respected them for it. How much more should we submit to the Father of our spirits and live! Our fathers disciplined us for a little while as they thought best; but God disciplines us for our good, that we may share in his holiness. No discipline seems pleasant at the time, but painful. Later on, however, it produces a harvest of righteousness and peace for those who have been trained by it.

The need for reassurance is real and deep. Life's difficulties are not the result of God's rejection—they might even be confirmation of our legitimacy.

MANY ROOMS

Although not every crisis in life is one of life-and-death proportion, we recognize that to pull us through, the anchors of our life
must be set in that which is eternal. Jesus moved from "Trust in God;
trust also in me" to "In my Father's house are many rooms." Our
hope in the temporal is anchored to the unseen and eternal realm
where we hold citizenship.

As we see our kedge anchors lined up on the deck of the ship,
we begin to see that while each is an important anchor, each one is
unique. Each has a role in kedging when we come to those *kairos*
moments. There is the anchor of our identity in Christ. There is the
anchor of knowing that God is in control of the circumstances. To
utilize those anchors that Jesus provides, we must take to heart his
admonition—trust in God and in what he has provided.

We can only imagine what happened the first time the captain
gave the order for kedging: "Take two anchors out in small boats
about half a mile. Drop the anchors into the water. Then the boat
will be pulled toward the anchors." The sailors must have scratched
their heads. Could this possibly work, or had the captain been into
the barrel of rum? The equipment was all there—the long boats, the
anchors, the rope. For kedging to work, the crew needed to obey the
captain, to accede to his admonition, "Follow my command, and
trust the process to work!"

I think of the untimely death of thirteen coal miners in West
Virginia in January 2006. It serves as a model of lives uniquely aware
and uniquely prepared every day for life's uncertainties. Coal miners, under no delusion of the risks they faced each day on the job,
gathered for prayer each morning before descending into the Sago
Mine—not a practice we see often in other workplaces. On the first
workday of the year, an explosion killed a miner and caused the rest
to flee to the end of the shaft. As their lives began to expire from the
carbon monoxide and carbon dioxide gases, the miners left notes for

loved ones. One read, "See you on the other side." It spoke of a man who lived daily by faith and who was able to pass through this worst-case scenario in his life by means of a well-established kedge. As his life was ending in that dark mine shaft a thousand feet below the surface, he was spiritually tied—as he had been each day he entered the mine—to an anchor that pulled him through his darkest hour. His anchor was set in his eternal hope in Jesus Christ, and it would pull him through to the other side.

10

ADMONITION 2:
WATCH OUT

(THE DANGERS OF PRIDE AND FOOLISHNESS)

REMEMBER THE WORDS I SPOKE TO YOU: "NO
SERVANT IS GREATER THAN HIS MASTER."

E ach disciple was struggling to process what Jesus was telling them. They had just witnessed talk of betrayal and Judas's departure; they would soon abandon Jesus and be scattered. He would no longer be with them. Peter would deny him three times. They were all over-whelmed emotionally. As if that were not enough—even more than they could bear—Jesus also used the occasion to teach the disciples for the first time about persecution and hatred. He had refrained from such a discussion previously because he had been with them. For most of the three years they had been with him, they rode the crest of a wave of popularity, and discussions of hatred and persecution might have seemed rather incongruous. Even though it would mean a second full dose of grief for them, Jesus took the occasion of the Last Supper to warn them of the new reality—that to belong to him and to be identi-fied with him might well result in hatred and persecution.

Our response to warnings is not always what it should be. Foolishness (as in believing something is unlikely ever to happen) together with pride (as in believing something could never happen to me) are a dangerous combination. One or both seem to be the responses we manifest when someone gives us a warning. We are not easily disposed to receiving advice, even though we know intellectually that to be forewarned is to be forearmed. While we don't know in detail how the Eleven responded when Jesus gave them advanced warning about the hatred and persecution to come, we do know that Peter vigorously repelled Jesus' suggestion that he might deny the Lord in the face of persecution—it might possibly happen to others, but could never happen to him. It was foolish of Peter to question anything Jesus told him by way of prediction, and it was prideful to deny that what Jesus predicted could happen to him.

As the infamous RMS *Titanic* was sinking on a cold April night in 1912, its equally infamous captain, Edward J. Smith, must have wondered how he could have been so foolish or so vain—or both. It was to have been (and would prove to be) his last voyage at the end of a distinguished career. He wanted a safe first cruise for *Titanic*, at all costs, while some representatives of the White Star Line wanted to break the record time for crossing the North Atlantic. Smith knew the risks of the North Atlantic in early spring better than anyone. He had been clearly warned of the risk of an ice floe. He seems, however, to have been caught up in a wave of folly—believing his ship was unsinkable. Then he seems to have been caught up in a wave of hubris—a collision with an iceberg could never happen to him. As the ship sank underneath him into the icy water, I have to wonder if he was more distressed by his foolishness (that any ship was truly unsinkable) or his pride (it could never happen to me). We will never know his last thoughts as he went down along with 1,517 souls that night.

Captain Smith's life and death provide us an important lesson:

When we fail to heed a warning, it is usually the result of folly or pride—or both. They do, after all, go closely together, as I learned painfully a couple years ago. Not many months after my daughter, Lauren, received her driver's license, I had the occasion to ride with her in her car. I had gone through the harrowing adventure of teaching a teenager to drive, so I had ridden with her many times before and thought she was an adequate driver. However, I was not prepared for my ride that afternoon. She drove too fast and was borderline reckless. I knew she would not remain "wreck-less" for long. I told her to slow down, and she reluctantly agreed, backing off the accelerator—for a while. As she dropped me off at my office, I said to her as lovingly as possible: "This is not how I taught you to drive. You need to slow down and drive much more cautiously. You need to drive defensively. You are an accident waiting to happen." Her response was less than I hoped for: "Yeah, yeah (patronizing tone)! But I'm a good driver (argumentative tone). You are worrying for no reason (conciliatory tone)."

Less than eight hours later, she took off after dinner to deliver a gift to a friend. Less than a mile from home, she didn't respond quickly enough to a light changing from green to red, and she broadsided another vehicle. The airbags deployed, and the front-end crumple zone crumpled as designed, saving her life but totaling her vehicle. When I arrived at the scene a few minutes later, I found a shaking and sobbing eighteen-year-old. In what may have been one of the great moments in the history of parental restraint, I refrained from saying the obvious. The foolishness and the pride of an eighteen-year-old—unwilling to heed the warning of her father and driving teacher—were the root cause of an accident. Three years later, I know the insurance company has not forgotten the accident because my insurance rates rival my mortgage! And I don't want her to forget it either, as a reminder of the dangers of foolishness and pride behind the wheel. Remembering how our pride and our foolishness prevent us from heeding warnings is foundational for processing Jesus' warning to his disciples (and his church) that persecution for the name of Christ is to be expected.

THE PRECEDENT

For those of us who increasingly love Jesus, it is not always easy to recognize just how much others hate him. He did nothing in his life that was sinful. He didn't lie. He wasn't arrogant or full of himself. He never cheated anyone. He didn't have an affair with another man's wife. He wasn't a bully or a petty gossip or an obnoxious drunk. He didn't corrupt others with influence peddling. He didn't behave in a way that we would think him a jerk (a universally understood but difficult to define word). In other words, he didn't do the usual kinds of things that would cause other people to hate him. In fact, in his daily conduct and communication, he manifested the qualities of patience, kindness, goodness, and selflessness that would cause most people to consider him a remarkably good person. As I recall Rick Warren saying to Larry King: "What's not to like about Jesus?"

Jesus told his closest friends that the world hated him: "If the world hates you, keep in mind that it hated me first" (John 15:18). The disciples might not have understood this very well. They had seen a great deal of public and private expressions of love and affirmation; and they might not have seen all the hatred brewing in the hearts of men as they plotted to kill Jesus. Or it is possible that they saw the conflict with the Pharisees and Sadducees but it really didn't register. They would, however, see within the next day the degree to which Jesus' enemies despised him, showing him the greatest degree of contempt and not the slightest measure of pity during his trial and agonizing death. It is of value for us to note why he was hated and how he responded to being hated.

HATED BY THE RELIGIOUS INSTITUTION

The chief priests and the rulers of the Jewish religious structure loathed him. Caiaphas and Annas despised him as a bright but uneducated and uncredentialed preacher who seriously threatened the existence of their very profitable industry, the temple, with its lucrative sacrificial system. Jesus wouldn't go along with this corrupt system, and the animosity of the Jewish leaders grew against him. As in *The Godfather* saga, the Jewish mafia became angry and resentful toward anyone who was an affront to their position and authority and extortive monetary gains.

The Pharisees uniquely hated Jesus because he challenged both their spiritual authority and their spiritual character. As early as the Sermon on the Mount, Jesus proposed a standard for entrance into the kingdom of heaven that implied that the Pharisees were not qualified: "For I tell you that unless your righteousness surpasses that of the Pharisees and the teachers of the law, you will certainly not enter the kingdom of heaven" (Matthew 5:20).

Of course the Pharisees would have been enraged by this. They did not understand that as for their patriarch Abraham, the only righteousness that satisfies God is the righteousness that God himself attributes to sinners who come to him by faith. True righteousness cannot be attained by human effort or the meticulous keeping of the law—to which the Pharisees had dedicated their lives. For Jesus to repudiate their righteousness was to deny their spiritual position in the kingdom of God and to challenge their spiritual condition in the community where they presumed to be leaders based on their strict observance of the law.

As we touched on in chapter 1, Jesus also repudiated their voluminous commentaries on Scripture. The heart of the Sermon on the Mount (Matthew 5:21–48) is a section of teaching that trumped the Jewish commentaries that had been the life work of the Pharisees and the teachers of the law. Repeatedly, Jesus used phrases such as, "You have heard that it was said . . ." and "But I tell you . . ." Jesus might just as well have said, "You have heard it from the Pharisees . . . but they are totally wrong and their teaching is bogus, as you will see from what I say." Again, he publicly challenged the Pharisees' spiritual authority in the community.

On several occasions the point of contention between Jesus and the Pharisees was the Sabbath. Jesus not only healed and did good on the Sabbath but he also proclaimed that "the Sabbath was made for man, not man for the Sabbath" (Mark 2:27). The Pharisees were especially concerned about the Sabbath because it was an outward expression of the covenantal relationship between God and Israel. In their understanding the faithful keeping of the Sabbath was a badge of honor for Israel as God's chosen people that had to be protected at all costs. Consequently, the Pharisees had in their commentaries devised and amassed hundreds of laws prescribing exactly what could and couldn't be done on the Sabbath. These constituted huge burdens that the Pharisees sought to impose on everyone in defense of the integrity of the Sabbath. Matthew 12 tells us that it was over a series of Sabbath controversies that for the first time the "Pharisees went out and plotted how they might kill Jesus" (v. 14).

The ongoing confrontations between the Pharisees and Jesus culminated in the remarkable account in Matthew 23 where Jesus publicly rebuked them:

> Then Jesus said *to the crowds* and to his disciples: "The teachers of the law and the Pharisees sit in Moses' seat. So you must obey them and do everything they tell you. But do not do what they do, for they do not practice what they preach. They tie up heavy loads and put them on men's shoulders, but they themselves are not willing to lift a finger to move them.
>
> *"Everything they do is done for men to see*: They make

their phylacteries wide and the tassels on their garments long; they love the place of honor at banquets and the most important seats in the synagogues; they love to be greeted in the marketplaces and to have men call them 'Rabbi.' . . .

"Woe to you, teachers of the law and Pharisees, you hypocrites! You shut the kingdom of heaven in men's faces. *You yourselves do not enter*, nor will you let those enter who are trying to.

"Woe to you, teachers of the law and Pharisees, you hypocrites! You travel over land and sea to win a single convert, and when he becomes one, you make him *twice as much a son of hell as you are*" (Matthew 23:1–15, emphasis added).

The Pharisees were clearly incensed by Jesus' words, certainly among the sternest words he ever spoke. He confronted them because they were responsible for teaching but proved to be blind guides who led others away from God to suffer eternal consequences.

HATED BY THE THEOLOGIANS

The Sadducees hated Jesus more on theological grounds, because he clearly taught the existence of a transcendent kingdom and with it the hope of resurrection to eternal life. In a debate on the issue of marriage in heaven, Jesus embarrassed the Sadducees publicly. They came to trap him with an absurd question about a woman who was widowed six times and as a result was married to seven brothers in succession. They asked Jesus whose wife she would be in heaven. Jesus humiliated them with his answer: "You are in error because you do not know the Scriptures or the power of God. At the resurrection people will neither marry nor be given in marriage; they will be like the angels in heaven. But about the resurrection of the dead—have you not read what God said to you, 'I am the God of Abraham, the

God of Isaac, and the God of Jacob'? He is not the God of the dead but of the living" (Matthew 22:29–32).

For the Sadducees who came seeking to paint Jesus into a corner, the exchange caused a significant public embarrassment instead. Jesus' blunt remark, "You are in error because you do not know the Scriptures," had to be a humiliating affront to their place as teachers of the law of God. We can imagine the ripples he caused by this public incident because of verse 34: "Hearing that Jesus had silenced the Sadducees, the Pharisees got together." A peasant preacher had publicly silenced them, and their pride was seriously wounded. The Sadducees found sufficient reason to hate Jesus that day, if they did not have reason before.

HATED BY THE SELF-RIGHTEOUS

Others hated Jesus because his righteousness simply made them aware of their own sinfulness. If the Holy Spirit was to continue Jesus' work of convicting the world of sin and righteousness and judgment, certainly we cannot overlook this aspect of Jesus' ministry. His mere presence caused some discomfort because he was perfect in his righteousness before God. The presence of a righteous person is a blinding light from which many retreat and which many resent. We prefer darkness to light because our deeds are evil (John 3:19).

I recall all-star professional basketball player A. C. Green (now retired) at the height of his basketball career appearing on a TV talk show. Although Green was an all-star and had two championship rings with the L. A. Lakers, it was his celibacy, not his celebrity, that was of interest to the host that day. Dramatically different from many other players who are philanderers (like Wilt Chamberlain, who once proudly claimed to have had sex with twenty thousand women during his career), Green was a virgin who had made a public statement that he would remain a virgin until he married. He repeated that declaration on the stage before a studio audience. At first the audience laughed; then they booed and jeered him. As the program host went into the audience for questions and comments, one woman stood and angrily asked, "Who do you think you are to judge the rest of us?" Curiously, Green had made no moral statement or remark that could have possibly been considered judgmental. He mentioned no other person or anyone else's behavior.[1] Obviously, the mere presence of a righteous person caused unrighteous people to be very uncomfortable to the point of anger. Jesus' mere presence, at least in some circles, must have caused many to be very uncomfortable and ultimately generated hatred toward him.

THE POSTURE

None of us relishes being criticized, disliked, rejected, or hated. Hatred is, of course, in a category of its own. Hate is an intense feeling that acts on the will; it is more than dislike on steroids. Jesus said there was really no difference between the person who hates and the person who hates and acts on that hatred. There is no internal difference between the volcano that erupts and the volcano alongside it that never erupts—both have cores of boiling magma. Most people do not easily accept the realization that someone hates them because hate is such an intense emotion. Jesus knew that certain people hated him, and he wanted the Eleven and us to know that when we belong to him, identify with him, and grow in his likeness, some will hate us as well.

Our natural inclination is to seek approval from others, sometimes at the cost of God's approval. It is curious that in one effort to trap Jesus, the Pharisees resorted to flattering Jesus at this very point: "Then the Pharisees went out and laid plans to trap him in his words. They sent their disciples to him along with the Herodians. "Teacher," they said, "we know you are a man of integrity and that you teach the way of God in accordance with the truth. *You aren't swayed by men, because you pay no attention to who they are.* Tell us then, what is your opinion? Is it right to pay taxes to Caesar or not?" (Matthew 22:15–17, emphasis added).

Jesus resisted their flattery and the temptation to compromise the truth—which they fully expected him to do in order to answer the question. But they were correct; Jesus paid no attention to the opinion of others. When we seek to please God rather than people, we always run the risk of a hostile response from dislike to disdain and all the way to hatred. That is why Jesus told his disciples, "If the world hates you, keep in mind that it hated me first" (John 15:18).

There is a matter-of-factness to Jesus' declaration. He seemed almost untouched by the realization, although he knew that the hatred of the Pharisees, the Sadducees, and the chief priests would soon be poured out on him. There was a unique (divine) perspective that allowed him to process this hate without needing to react to it.

First, there was no self-defensive explanation or excuse on Jesus' part. He had done nothing wrong and had not sinned against anyone. Yet he acknowledged that they hated him because of the message that he taught, which they refused to receive. They hated him also for the miracles he performed because those validated the teaching they refused to receive. His eyes were wide open. If he had not taught what he taught and not done the miracles that he did, they would not have hated him (John 15:22–24). Being hated is a natural consequence of speaking the truth about God and about the unseen kingdom of God.

Second, Jesus was able to cope with the irrational nature of hatred. They hated him "without reason" (v. 25), or we might say, without adequate reason. Jesus knew they hated him because of his teaching and his miracles, but certainly his miracles were not a sufficient and rational reason to hate him. He had not sinned against them, but he did expose their sin to them.

I have recently learned some painful lessons about hate from my own heart and the distinction between hating with cause and hating without cause. Bear with me here as I give an example from a movie I watched.

Not long ago I went to see an outstanding but disturbing film, *The Great Raid*. The film retells the historical account of the American soldiers who surrendered to the Japanese forces in World War II on the island of Corregidor in the Philippines. The Japanese deeply believed that surrender was dishonorable, something they would never do (and as the war would reveal, many did take their own lives rather than surrender). As a result, they loathed the American troops who surrendered to them. Their contempt—even hatred—of these Americans resulted in the cruel Bataan Death March north through the Bataan peninsula to prisoner of war camps. Hundreds died on the way, as the Japanese captors starved and dehydrated their prisoners and then bayoneted those who could not keep up. In the three prison camps, the Americans were maliciously mistreated in gross violation of the rules of war. As the tide of war in the Philippines turned with the return of General McArthur and the Allied forces, the Japanese forces unleashed even greater cruelty on their captives. Committed to never allowing these despised Americans to be released as the liberating American forces approached the camps, the Japanese in one camp herded all the prisoners into underground air-raid shelters. There they barricaded the exit, poured gasoline in over them, and set them on fire. When the Allied forces reached the camp and realized what the Japanese had done to their prisoners, plans were quickly drawn up for a surprise raid to liberate the other camps before the captors could repeat this barbaric act. So the great raid was planned that liberated the third camp and saved hundreds of lives there.

I am extremely sensitive to and respond strongly to injustice. I left the theater deeply distressed and agitated. I told my friend, "The old nature in me wants to go out and do something violent to the first Japanese person I see." I didn't, of course. I love the Japanese people—I initiated a Japanese church plant as a pastor and know from my visits to Japan that the Japanese people have grieved deeply over the sins of that era. Yet, I had to process that very powerful emotion. What I felt was hate, but it was not "without cause," I told myself. Was I not reacting to the cruelty and inhumanity of the Japanese soldiers of that era? But how could I say that I was merely "hating the sin" when I focused these strong feelings on certain people? Is it not justifiable to hate (with cause) those who (like the Japanese) hate without cause and treat others with such cruelty? Is it not in some small way like the wrath of God—the eternal disposition of God toward sin? Is there, then, a difference between hate with good cause (sin) and hate without cause? Am I to respond to both equally? I attempted to distinguish in my mind "hating without cause" and a similar and equal emotional reaction prompted by the sin of others.

Being hated is difficult enough to deal with. Being hated without cause is a greater emotional challenge, because if we have done nothing wrong, there is not only hatred to deal with but also the accompanying sense of injustice. Jesus acknowledged, "They hate me without cause." There was no plea or protest about being misunderstood or wrongly judged or the obvious injustice that was beginning to rain down on him. It was simply an acknowledgment of the reality; and Jesus modeled for his disciples the ability to process being hated without cause, which is to be hated unjustly. Everything he would endure in the next hours was unjust. To be able to endure the unjust hate depended on his ability to process the reality that they hated him without cause.

A third feature of Jesus' divine perspective on hate was his ability to differentiate the hate from the haters. He was able the next day to utter history's unmatched words, "Father, forgive them, for they do not know what they are doing." Jesus knew that they hated him, that they hated him without cause, and that their hatred was rooted in ignorance. How could anyone fully understand that "God so loved the world that he gave his one and only Son" and truly hate with reason and with cause? In this we marvel most at Jesus' capacity to hate the sin without hating the sinner. All of this ties together when we recognize that his capacity to love the sinner while hating the sin makes the question of cause irrelevant. When you are able to hate the sin without hating the sinner, then it really doesn't matter if they hate you with sufficient cause or unjustly without cause.

THE POIGNANT PROMISE

Because no servant is greater than his master, we who are servants of Jesus Christ should not be surprised that people will hate us. That was the next vital part of Jesus' message to the disciples, and it served as a clear advance warning. We would be foolish to say it could not happen; and we would be arrogant to say it could never happen to us. It is some combination of foolishness and pride to be surprised when we are hated for the sake of Christ.

As I mentioned before, I teach philosophy as an adjunct professor at a secular state school. One of the reasons I took this low-paying, part-time job (think minimum wage) is that I want to spend part of my life outside the cocoon of the Christian subculture, a pretty large subculture in Colorado Springs where I live. A philosophy class provides a unique forum for people to talk about their worldviews. Early in the semester, most of my students have not yet gathered enough information to discover that I am a Christian. As a result, early class sessions are marked by some very open and hostile remarks about Christianity from a handful of students. I have heard Christianity, and therefore Christians, called silly, stupid, inconsistent, diabolical (as if the student knew the true meaning), and oppressive. I've heard the Bible referred to as bullshit or worse. Although there may be some exercise of student restraint after they discover my identity and spiritual orientation (restraint that is motivated, I suppose, by a desire not to offend the teacher and all powerful grade giver), early on it pours out quite freely without any regard, even for the possible presence of a Christian classmate who might take offense.

I entertain the thought that if they only knew me—how good and loving a person I am, how well-educated I am, how well I have thought through the case for Christianity, and how much more deeply I have thought about these life issues than they—then they would esteem me as a teacher and respect my reasoned perspectives. I hope that because I am different from some stereotypes with which they entered the class, I might enable them to get beyond those. So I harbor the illusion that if I demonstrate that I am open-minded and not typical of their stereotypes of Christians (a Bible-banging mother-in-law in one case, a very legalistic parent in another), then they will embrace, or at least become tolerant of, Christianity. Perhaps my good deeds will cause some to glorify my Father in heaven. I hope my illusion will become reality, and I pray that it will; but I am already convinced that it is not likely.

It is evident that two thousand years after Jesus' warning, some of my students will hate me simply because I am a servant of Jesus. The manifestation of that hatred may well be kept somewhat in check because of my position of authority and the near-magical power of the grade that I give, but make no mistake—the animosity is visible right below the surface, waiting for opportunities, like a philosophy class, to burst forth like a volcano.

As a teacher, I acknowledge the temptation to seek the approval of people rather than God. So I must remind myself as I walk into class that while I am called to do good works that might cause some to glorify God, that is different than doing good works (of kindness, tolerance, fairness, even good teaching) so that my students will like me. I sense the temptation to talk about those "other Christians"—the narrow-minded and right-wing fundamentalists who stir up animosity and reinforce the stereotypes—as belonging to a different group than mine. But as an evangelical I believe as the fundamentalists do about the Bible and the exclusive nature of the claims of Christ. So while I see a clear attitudinal distinction, there exists little theological distinction. Because I consider gay marriage an oxymoron but less a problem than the global AIDS crisis, and while I consider abortion wrong but less a problem than poverty and injustice, my students will find it easy to lump me together with those who are so overtly hostile toward homosexuality or whose rhetoric about abortion never retreats from a fevered pitch. I am less than certain, then, that a group of freshmen philosophy students are capable of grasping the nuances of how a pedigreed, progressive evangelical is different from a dyed-in-the-wool, right-wing fundamentalist.

Of course, some Christians especially give all of Christianity bad publicity, and some talking heads among the ranks of Christians are an embarrassment. But we are foolish and proud to seek to distance ourselves from "those Christians" or to think that the average non-Christian could perhaps understand the difference. We are foolish and proud if we think it is our responsibility or within our ability to put a better face on Jesus or a better spin on Christianity, whether we are teaching philosophy on a secular college campus or seeking somehow to make Christianity more palatable to a whole generation of postmoderns, as some seem to be trying to do.

THE WORST-CASE SCENARIO

As I noted in an earlier chapter, Ralph Stice's *From 9/11 to 666* spells out a very chilling *possible* scenario that anticipates the rise of an Islamic antichrist (the Twelfth Imam of Islamic prophecy, regarded by some as the Islamic messiah), possibly in the next decade. Of course much of Islam rejects radicalism (and the Jihadist movement) and does not believe it will achieve its goals in the Islamic community or the world. And while we cannot presume to predict future events, the rise of militant Islam (and the mere possibility of militants obtaining nuclear weapons), with its increased hostility toward

I can certainly hope there is a pretribulation rapture and the *Left Behind* series is dead on target. Or I can cast my lot with the amillennialists who believe that most of Revelation is about the persecution of the church by the Roman Empire, or with the postmillennialists who believe that the gospel will continue to advance and that the church will triumphantly usher in the kingdom of God on earth. But in light of the utter lack of agreement among the many evangelical scholars with better credentials than mine, it appears that there is no way to be certain about the "day of the Lord." As a result, I have determined to be wise and humble in response to Jesus' words of warning about persecution. I think it foolish and proud not to prepare for the worst-case scenario among the various eschatological positions.

Marvin J. Rosenthal postulated what may well be the *worst-case* scenario in his earthshaking work, *The Pre-Wrath Rapture of the Church*.[2] According to Rosenthal's premillenial perspective, the church of Jesus will be spared the wrath of God but will not be spared the tribulation of the last days. (Good so far, in light of the clear distinction between wrath and tribulation.) Rosenthal then, if I read him correctly, focused on a short window of time between the end of the three-and-a-half years of tribulation and the commencement of God's wrath to be poured out from seven bowls (Revelation 16). He posited that near the middle point of the seven years of the tribulation, the ministry of the two prophets in Jerusalem (Revelation 11) will finally come to an end after 1,260 days. These two witnesses, who have been protected by God for those forty-two months, will be stripped of their protection and quickly slain by a world that hates them and has wanted to kill them from the time their ministry began. A widespread celebration following their deaths will include the

214

exchange of gifts, much like Christmas. Their corpses, according to Revelation, will lie in the street for three days, when suddenly they will be resurrected and taken up to heaven. Following this, the seventh trumpet will sound and the final countdown sequence of world history will begin, unleashing the wrath of God.

However, while the two witnesses' bodies remain in the street of Jerusalem, and just before the wrath of God is poured out on the world, there will come a time of great tribulation for all the believers on earth. Jesus described it in the Olivet Discourse in Matthew:

> Then you will be handed over to be *persecuted* and put to death, and you will be *hated by all nations because of me.* At that time many will *turn away* from the faith and will betray and hate each other, and many false prophets will appear and deceive many people. Because of the increase of wickedness, the love of most will grow cold, but he who stands firm to the end will be saved. And this gospel of the kingdom will be preached in the whole world as a testimony to all nations, and then the end will come.
>
> So when you see standing in the holy place 'the abomination that causes desolation,' spoken of through the prophet Daniel—let the reader understand—then let those who are in Judea flee to the mountains. . . . For then there will be great distress, *unequaled from the beginning of the world until now—and never to be equaled again. If those days had not been cut short, no one would survive, but for the sake of the elect those days will be shortened.* . . . See, I have told you ahead of time (Matthew 24:9–25, emphasis added).

It appears to some, then, that when the protection is taken off the two witnesses in Jerusalem and they are killed, that Christians all over the world will be left without protection and need to hide.

Many, many will be killed. These are the days that will be shortened. Had these days not been shortened, then no believers would survive. Following these unprecedented days of tribulation, the wrath of God will be poured out on the world that has just inflicted carnage on the bride of Christ. The rapture of the church, then, will not come until after some time of global genocide so awful that no believer would have survived had the church not been spared its full duration.

Whether you agree with this eschatology or not, I think you may agree that it spells out a worst-case scenario of the end times.

Jesus warned us that hatred and resulting tribulation would come to his followers because no servant is greater than his master. It is foolish and proud not to be prepared for anything less than the worst-case scenario. That is why Jesus told the Eleven that night, "All this I have told you so that you will not go astray. . . . I have told you this, so that when the time comes you will remember that I warned you" (John 16:1–4).

According to church history, followers of Jesus Christ have suffered hatred and its accompanying persecution from the time of Stephen forward. Stephen's death (Acts 7) was followed by that of the apostle James, and persecution ultimately came to all those gathered in the upper room that night. There have been millions since.

Numbers are inexact, but it may well be that more Christians died for their faith in the 20th century than all the prior centuries since Stephen. Estimates vary, but somewhere between 160,000 and 200,000 Christians will die for their faith this year—most in the 10–40 window—even as the church in this region of the world continues to expand dramatically. And although I do not now live in a high-risk setting as others do, I would be foolish and arrogant to assume that my environment will remain unchanged or that such hatred and persecution would pass over my house. There is no special lamb's blood on the doorposts and lintel of my door. Our only protection is given to us by the blood of the Lamb: the hope of eternal life should we be forced to face the sword. It only makes sense for each believer to prepare for a worst-case scenario for the future—just in case Marv Rosenthal happened to get it right.

I write this paragraph on the fiftieth anniversary of the death of five missionaries slain in Ecuador. I remember the event and recall seeing the images in *Life* magazine. I've had the privilege over the years to meet members of the families of the five. I have read numerous articles and accounts of the martyrs. I recall reading Jim Elliot's journal, in which he expressed willingness, even desire, to give his life for Jesus Christ. I've wondered why a man with such a desire, who wrote that he had no remaining aspirations in this world, would have chosen to marry. Yet I am aware that the death of Jim Elliot and the others launched a whole generation of missionaries onto the mission field. More than twenty fliers from the United States promptly applied to take Nate Saint's place. More than a thousand college students volunteered for foreign missions in direct response to the story of these five martyrs. There was no foolishness or pride in the heart of Jim Elliott who famously told his generation, "He is no fool who gives up what he cannot keep to gain that which he cannot lose."

A generation later, in an age many of us heard Francis Schaeffer describe as one taken up with the primary values of "personal peace and affluence," I wonder if the death of five young missionaries would have quite the same impact on the church today. Fortunately, there is a wave of young believers who are sold out to the cause of Christ and are preparing for such a calling, but how many in the North American church are concerned primarily about the quality of their coming retirement? If I consider the worst-case scenario for just a moment, then I must acknowledge that my life may be cut short as a martyr in an increasingly violent world. But this is a harsh reality and not at all in keeping with the era of felt needs and feel-good preaching.

Jesus warned us so that we would not go astray when difficulties—whether trials or tribulation—come calling. My memory banks are filled with faces and names of people who have gone astray when disaster crashed into their lives. I think particularly of two couples, out of several I have counseled, who lost a young child. One was a missionary couple in Africa who lost their first child, a son, when he was only weeks old. Their son was born prematurely and soon developed a hernia that needed repair. Carried on a motorbike to the nearest hospital, he did not survive. The great crisis of their faith ("God, we trusted that if you called us to Africa you would protect us") was intensified by the ignorant comments of fellow missionaries that their son died because "there must be some sin" in their lives. Their faith was rocked, and they nearly went astray. I consider it a great ministry moment when I was able to help them hold on to their faith. Today they are back in Africa with their four children, serving at an orphanage.

The second memory is of a staff member and his wife who lost a first child due to SIDS. When they lost their son, they drew closer to God than ever before, finding comfort and assurance. Their response stands in sharp contrast to many others (like Ted Turner, mentioned earlier) who say they turned away from God after the tragic death of a child or some other devastating difficulty.

We are warned as believers not to be surprised when difficulties—whether trials or tribulation—come into our lives and not to go astray because of them. Remember Jesus' warning: "All this I have told you so that you will not go astray. . . . I have told you this, so that when the time comes you will remember that I warned you." This is an important and useful kedge to pull us through difficult times. But we have to be willing to use a kedge; we have to take his warning to heart.

11

LINKING OUR ANCHORS
AND JESUS' ADMONITIONS

I HAVE MUCH MORE TO SAY TO YOU, MORE THAN YOU
CAN NOW BEAR.

The Farewell Discourse provides no cookbook approach to life and its anticipated crises. The way through the turbulent waters of life is not found on a map but by staying close to the one who can navigate and guide us because he himself passed through the greatest storm. Certainly, the five anchors are really no surprise: grasp firmly who you are in Christ; clutch with both hands that he is in control at all times; use four fingers and your thumb to grip the truth of God's Word; hold on to the braided cord of prayer; and become thoroughly entangled in the Holy Spirit. But learning these truths and learning kedging when the skies and the seas are calm is not always our practice. The wisdom of Solomon would advise us to pay attention to these matters "before the days of trouble come" (Ecclesiastes 12:1). Unfortunately, in the relative comfort of our North American environment, we tend to demonstrate the same approach we have to keeping emergency supplies at home, regularly changing batteries in smoke detectors, and keeping the first aid kit stocked.

We are not always spiritually, emotionally, and psychologically prepared for trouble. So with the anchors come the admonitions Jesus gave to the Eleven that night: learn to trust God—to really trust God, and don't proudly presume for a moment that you are immune to a great storm in your life. And he added a thought that is so curious because it is at the same time chilling and comforting: "I have much more to say to you, more than you can now bear" (John 16:12).

It is chilling because Jesus reminded the Eleven that there would come times of overwhelming circumstances. The disciples were right on the edge that night and would reveal their emotional exhaustion in the garden. The next day would certainly bring more than most of us can comprehend as they watched their master and their friend scourged and crucified.

Perhaps nothing approximates that level of "more than you can now bear" as the loss of a child or the loss of a spouse. In my years of pastoral ministry, I witnessed people so overwhelmed with grief that they needed sedation.

William was a West Virginian who had accumulated many very hard miles in his sixty years. He looked more like a man in his late seventies. We met when I was serving as a volunteer chaplain at a Los Angeles–area hospital. Pastors from the area took one night a month and did a 6 p.m. to 6 a.m. shift, and this was my night. William was having surgery for cancer of the mouth the next day. It was his third such surgery for cancer, and much of his face and jaw and lips had been removed the first two times. Severely disfigured, he didn't go out in public much. It had been many months since I had seen him when his wife called me sounding deeply distressed. I assumed from the first sounds of the call that William had died, but I was wrong; his son Billy had died. He had taken his own life at age thirty-four when his wife left him. He shot himself with a shotgun and then died several painful days later in the hospital, ultimately of peritonitis. I went to their modest home later that day and found a family beyond consolation.

They asked me to officiate at Billy's funeral. I agreed, somewhat reluctantly because I had never met Billy. I was not prepared for the outpouring of grief I saw that day at the funeral home. At the close of the service, as the thirty or so mourners filed past the closed casket, William was last in line. As he approached the casket of his son, he threw himself on top of it, sending the floral spray to the floor. There he hugged the casket, sobbing and wailing the name of his son repeatedly. Only after several very uncomfortable moments did the staff of the funeral home come and tactfully assist him off and away from the bier. Fortunately, there was no graveside service, as the body was donated to science. I had seen grief before; I had experienced grief myself. But never had I encountered grief like this.

C. S. Lewis, the great Christian apologist whom we might assume had an answer for every question, nearly came apart and lost his faith in the face of the death of his wife, Joy. In his remarkably revealing journal of grief published as *A Grief Observed*, Lewis wrote:

> No one ever told me that grief felt so like fear.
>
> Your bid—for God or no God, for a good God or the Cosmic Sadist, for eternal life or nonentity—will not be serious if nothing much is staked on it. And you will never discover how serious it was until the stakes are raised horribly high.
>
> Nothing will shake a man—or at any rate a man like me—out of his merely verbal thinking and his merely notional beliefs. He has to be knocked silly before he comes to his senses. Only torture will bring out the truth. Only under torture does he discover it himself.[1]

Just as the disciples faced a terrible storm that night and the next day, we can anticipate encountering "more than you can now bear" crises, crises that drive us to the core of our being. God allows us to be "knocked silly" so that we find out where the anchors truly are. Lewis reminds us that this is serious business even as he acknowledged how unprepared he was, emotionally and spiritually.

While this is chilling, it is also comforting. Jesus knew the disciples' limits; and while there was more he might have said, he spared them so they would not be overwhelmed. The sovereign one who is with us knows what we can endure without him, and what we can endure with him.

Promises of God's presence even in the valleys on our journey are found throughout Scripture: "The LORD your God is with you, he is mighty to save. He will take great delight in you, he will quiet you with his love, he will rejoice over you with singing" (Zephaniah 3:17).

What is remarkable about Jesus' statement at this juncture is what it reveals: Jesus was intensely focused on the trials facing his disciples (rather than his own) and the grief the disciples were experiencing (rather than his own). He earnestly wanted to share the Passover that evening to prepare them, equipping them for what was coming. He was not focused on his own *kairos* moment, but on theirs, because he was already prepared and they were not yet. He had prepared for that storm his whole life, and they had not.

PRECEDENT FOR PREPARATION

Jesus was prepared for his *kairos* moment. Jesus had been tested by Satan many times, but his three distinct temptations in the wilderness uniquely prepared him for the great trial of the cross that awaited him.

- He learned the absolute priority of the spiritual realm over the earthly realm.
- He learned to stay on the difficult path and not take a shortcut.

- He learned the discipline of not calling on the angels of heaven to come to his aid.

Previously we noted that Jesus had a fully developed sense of who he was when, early in the evening, he washed the disciples' feet. Only people totally secure in their identity can serve others without a sense of loss or status or a blow to their pride. We also learned that Jesus knew that he came from God and was returning to God. His lifetime of growing self-awareness brought him to a level of absolute certainty that he was God in human form. He also knew that God had put all things under his authority, resulting in perhaps the most remarkable arrest sequence one could imagine.

Jesus told his disciples that they needed to know the distinction between belief in a transcendent God and belief in him, Jesus, the imminent and incarnate God. It is through Christ that God makes himself fully known and through Christ that he invites us to enter into a relationship with him. We've looked at how each of us has a struggle with faith in God because of a God distortion that is commensurate with our personality type. It is through our knowledge of Jesus that we are able to begin to correct our God distortions.

In his declaration that he is the Vine and we are the branches, Jesus clears the air and resolves all the questions about our identity, which is found through our relationship with our Creator and Redeemer. As a result, God's paradigm for health begins at a different point and runs in an opposite direction to those living according to the world's principles. We do not find our acceptance through our identity arrived at by physical accomplishments and material acquisitions. God has already accepted us because of the Word of God we have heard and received by faith. A life of fruitfulness for God and for his kingdom—the abundant life—will allow us to share in his great joy and know it as our own.

The subject of Jesus' departure caused great grief among the disciples. He promised them that he would return to be with them in the person of the Holy Spirit, as he would no longer be with them physically. The Holy Spirit would be different in his ubiquitous manifestation but just like Jesus in the role he would perform in our lives and in the world.

Because we belong to Jesus, we should not be surprised when hatred and persecution invade our lives. Jesus warned his disciples so that they would be prepared and not lose faith. Although Jesus had spoken extensively about sharing in his joy and the comfort of the Holy Spirit, he needed to prepare them for the persecution to come. We considered the "worst-case scenario" because if we are prepared for the worst, we should be able to navigate and pull through the difficulties of life with the kedges that Jesus provided his disciples.

In addition to the presence of the Holy Spirit leading us into truth, Jesus also provided a new dimension of prayer for his servants. For those who recognize that they are in a spiritual war, Jesus provides special access to the Father through his own name. Battlefield communication in the name of Jesus has special priority with the Father, our commanding officer. God knows our physical needs and has promised to provide for those needs with standard, daily prayer. But for those seeking to fulfill the Great Commission and encountering a hostile world in the process, prayer in Jesus' name has been provided for strategic help and to coordinate the spiritual attack of the kingdom as it advances.

And lastly, the truth of God's Word is an essential anchor for us in a world of relativism. While God does speak in many ways and Jesus said he had spoken figuratively, there are clear propositional statements in the Word of God that provide a set of guardrails for us to rightly understand all of the variously expressed truths of the Bible.

What a remarkable portrait begins to emerge as we put these pieces into place—a portrait of a person who gave to his disciples a portion of the peace that he himself was experiencing. In Jesus we see a man

- who loved and cared for his closest friends right to the end;
- with a fully developed self-awareness;
- who knew who he was and was able, therefore, to serve his friends by humbly washing their feet without any threat to his own identity;
- who had clearly established the absolute priority of the spiritual realm over the fleshly realm in his life;
- who was totally committed never to taking the path of expedience as he lived in obedience to God the Father;
- who had developed the unique discipline and restraint necessary not to call on the angels of heaven to rescue him from his difficult mission;
- who knew that all things were under his authority and was able to orchestrate the details of his own arrest, trial, and crucifixion;
- saturated with the Word of God, turning to its truth at every turn;
- able to see the ultimate joy at the end of the suffering;
- who prayed;
- who knew all his life when, where, and how he would die because he had embraced the cross as his life's purpose;
- who could say, "I have overcome the world";
- who experienced the peace of God that transcends human understanding and was able to give others a measure of his own peace.

This was a man who by the power of God operating freely in his life (and without the problem of sin) bore lasting fruit for God—he purchased men for God from every tribe and language and people and nation. He is the one who had a world of peace in a world breaking into pieces all around him. As we draw near in awe of his fully matured human character, we learn from him how to pass through our crises with a growing measure of peace. Everything Jesus taught the disciples that night, and taught us by extension, was not so that we might escape trouble but find his peace in the middle of our trouble: "I have told you these things, so that in me you may have peace."

We live in a world marked by trials, tribulation, and persecution for the followers of Jesus as well as marked by sickness, disease, disasters, and accompanying suffering that is the common lot of all who live in a fallen world. Knowing this, I am drawn again to the earlier story of Ed Landry, who clearly experienced God's presence and peace in a world falling to pieces. Ed had come to a *kairos* moment. Life as he knew it would nearly cease as he entered the cancer ward for thirty days of treatment while everyone else went about their routines. Of course, he was unable to work and unable to do anything he had planned to do to advance the kingdom of God while he lay there for a month—his new ministry in Nepal just wasn't going to happen. Yet his identity and the resulting eternal future were secure—not based on accomplishments (he had none) or appearance (you can imagine how he looked) or what he possessed (missionaries don't have much). He knew that his cancer was not punishment from God for his sin, but that God could use this time in his life to refine him even further and draw him even closer. The Word of God that he had memorized and others read to him was burning with power in his heart—these were no routine quiet times. The presence of God was real and rich—complete with the sense of being hugged by the Holy Spirit. Of course, there was no crash course Ed could have taken to prepare for that month in the hospital. He had learned as a branch in the years before how to abide in the Vine, and now it was time to take the exam. What is clear is that this ordeal did serve to prepare him for yet another month-long stay in the cancer ward, and even to anticipate another experience of God's adequacy in the middle of his tribulation.

"Trading Places: Cancer Ward" is one reality show that might have no applicants. Certainly, no one signs up for such suffering in order to experience the presence and peace of God. Unlike Jesus' life, we rarely have any indication when trials and tribulation are around the next corner.

In one sense, nothing can fully prepare us for myelogenous leukemia, breast cancer, a debilitating auto accident, or in my case sarcoidosis granuloma, so there is really no special preparation. How can anyone prepare for the cruel loss of a job, the death of a spouse or child, or a devastating financial setback? We cannot know—even as Job likely never knew—whether the crises we face are simply part of living in a sinful, fallen world or a specific attack of the evil one. James Boice was correct in noting that in either case—whether it originates with the fury of the evil one or the futility of the fallen world—nothing comes into our lives without our heavenly Father's knowledge. He is never surprised. In fact, he allows both, and he instructs us to "give thanks in all circumstances, for this is God's will for you in Christ Jesus (1 Thessalonians 5:18).

PREPARING OURSELVES

So while it is not possible to be prepared for all the contingencies of life, we can, however, be prepared in the all-important general sense for whatever is around the corner. As Jesus concluded his discourse, he said: "In this world you will have trouble. But take heart! I have overcome the world."

We marvel at Jesus' capacity to encounter his own passion with such maturity and health. His model provides us great assurance that as he speaks to us through the words of John 13–16 he knows at every level the reality of what he wants to teach us.

First, we prepare by taking the warning of Jesus to heart: In this world we will have trouble. Jesus offered no exemption or deferment and no explanation beyond the hate that people have for him and the reality that we live in a fallen (and still falling!) world. It is foolish and proud to believe otherwise.

Second, we prepare for whatever is around the corner by giving thanks for all those things—large and small. The reason for this is simple and foundational. Whenever we give thanks to God for anything, we take a step in his direction. Whenever we do not give thanks on all occasions, we take a step back from God. As I take even a single step closer to God, I hear his voice more distinctly; but as I take even a single step away from God, his voice becomes more distant.

Third, "Take heart," Jesus said. To take heart is to be encouraged and to acknowledge that everything that does come around the next corner of our lives was scrutinized by the top inspector, our Father in heaven. He promised not to allow a monstrous difficulty—one beyond our ability to cope—to come into our lives. So we take heart that God knows and controls the traffic on all the on-ramps of our lives.

Fourth, we prepare by drawing near. He has already overcome the world and left a trail marked out through the path of adversity he took, the one marked "worst-case scenario." As we follow close behind, working to put our feet into the footprints he placed on the path, we will be strengthened by our sense of identity in Christ, learn better how to pray, and take a firmer grip on the roadmap of God's Word. As we consciously breathe in the Spirit and breathe out self, the cord of the Holy Spirit entangles and envelops us.

Fifth, we must recognize and acknowledge that drawing near does not always resolve the existential moment. Hebrews 11 speaks of those who "gained what was promised" but then notes:

> Others were tortured and refused to be released, so that they might gain a better resurrection. Some faced jeers and flogging, while still others were chained and put in prison. They were stoned; they were sawed in two;

they were put to death by the sword. They went about
in sheepskins and goatskins, destitute, persecuted and
mistreated—the world was not worthy of them. They
wandered in deserts and mountains, and in caves and
holes in the ground.

These were all commended for their faith, *yet none
of them received what had been promised.* God had
planned something better for us so that only together
with us would they be made perfect. (vv. 35–40, emphasis added).

That is the great challenge of our faith—holding on by faith
when God does not seem present, because by faith we know that he
is and that he will not forsake his children. It is in those moments
that the tempter whispers in our ear: "If you really are a child of God,
what are you doing here in this barren place?"

Evidence Not Seen tells the story of a young American missionary
to the Dutch East Indies just before World War II. Taken captive,
she endured four years in notorious Japanese prison camps. Darlene
Rose tells how God sustained her through those four years—which
included beatings, illness, and her husband's death—sustained her
with a very real sense of his presence, just as my friend Ed Landry
described.

But Darlene also wrote of times when there was no sense of
God's presence at all when she was in solitary confinement and severely malnourished:

Quite suddenly and unexpectedly, I felt enveloped
in a spiritual vacuum. "Lord, where have You gone?
Why have You withdrawn Your presence from me? O
Father—" In panic I jumped to my feet, my heart frantically searching for a hidden sin, for a careless thought,
for any reason why my Lord should have withdrawn
his presence from me. My prayers, my expressions of

worship, seemed to go no higher than the ceiling; there seemed to be no sounding board. I prayed for forgiveness, for the Holy Spirit to search my heart. To none of my petitions was there any apparent response.

After crying to the Lord all night, Darlene came to a new understanding that she described this way:

> "Lord, I believe all that the Bible says. I do walk by faith and not by sight. I do not need to *feel* You near, because Your Word says You will never leave me nor forsake me. Lord, I confirm my faith; I believe." The words of Hebrews 11:1 welled up, unbeckoned, to fill my mind: "Now faith is the substance of things hoped for, *the evidence of things not seen.*" . . . Evidence not seen—that was what I put my trust in—not in feelings or moments of ecstasy, but in the unchanging Person of Jesus Christ. . . .
>
> In a measure I felt that I understood what Job meant when he declared, "Though He slay me, yet will I trust in Him" (13:15). Job knew that he could trust God, because Job knew the character of the One in Whom he had put his trust. It was faith stripped of feelings, faith without trappings.[2]

My ongoing crisis may not be as dramatic as Ed Landry's or as extreme as Darlene Rose's, but I have been coping with my *kairos* moment that has now lasted for four years. I am on permanent disability. I am limited by my need to be on supplemental oxygen twenty-four hours a day. I'm taking powerful immunosuppressant drugs to retard the advance of the disease, but it is relentless, slowly advancing. My preaching-ministry career has been dismantled, and I am learning to serve God primarily at a keyboard rather than behind a pulpit. I am being diminished a bit a time, having had the occasional cry as I discover there is something else I can no longer do.

I think at times that if I had known what was around the next corner, that might have been "more than you can now bear." And after all, that is not how life works. Nothing is announced ahead of time, and there is no à la carte of difficulties to choose from. But as we have thanked God each day, he has been there—providing peace at every step, together with miracles at critical moments along the way.

I think daily about dying and wonder how long before the disease overtakes me. I was encouraged by a recent e-mail from a lifelong friend and mentor: "My prayer is, Lord, keep bringing me 'home,' imagining the day when 'face to face' will be the norm. I'm ready."

I think daily about maintaining my grip on the anchors that Jesus supplies: who I am in Christ, knowing a loving Father is in control, grasping truth from God's Word, inviting the presence of the Holy Spirit into my life, and learning to pray all over again.

I try to think daily about his admonitions: Trust in the hope of an eternal home with Christ. Set your anchor there. Avoid the proud "Why me?" questions. The Farewell Discourse is not a recipe for navigating crises. It is ours to feed on.

Your *kairos* moments may not be like mine. Yet may the insights I have shared in these pages equip you with all of the anchors God has provided to encourage you on your journey. We have been given everything we need for life and godliness, so may all of Christ's followers find in him a world of peace when their world is falling to pieces.

Appendix 1

Excerpt from *Who Put My Life on Fast-Forward? How to Slow Down and Start Living Again* by Phil Callaway

Doug and Margaret Nichols have faced their share of obstacles. After surgery for colon cancer, Doug sat across from his doctor and listened in disbelief. "I'm sorry, Doug," said the doctor nervously, "but you do have a 30 percent chance of recovery."

"You mean I have a 70 percent chance of dying?" asked Doug, with a grin.

"I wouldn't put it that way," said a surprised doctor. "But my best estimate is that you have about three months to live."

"Well, let me tell you something, Doc," said Nichols. "Whatever happens, I have a 100 percent chance of going to heaven."

One year later radiation and chemo treatments had left Doug's body wracked with pain. Though he kept his humor well-oiled, both Doug and Margaret knew the end might be near. But their world was not the only one collapsing. Nightly news reports from Rwanda indicated that civil war had spiraled out of control and more than a million people had been slaughtered, many by their own neighbors and trusted friends. The carnage was beyond belief. Terrified Rwandans by the thousands had fled across the border into Zaire and crowded into filthy, ill-equipped refugee camps, where diseases such as cholera found a ready home. People were dying everywhere, 50,000 in three days alone in the little town of Goma.

As Margaret and Doug read the terrible accounts and saw the images on TV, their hearts were broken. But what could one couple do?

"I knew I was going to die," Doug told me, "but I wanted to do something before leaving this earth. I just wanted to hold some of those children in my arms and try to offer hope."

Soon Doug found himself traveling with a team of doctors and nurses through the heart of Rwanda, with no idea of the adventure that lay ahead.

A Rwandan Christian leader whom Doug had worked with before had hired three hundred refugees as stretcher-bearers to bury the daily masses of dead and transport the sick so doctors could do their best. One day the leader approached Doug with an expression of deep concern. "Mr. Nichols," he said, "we have a problem."

"What is it?" Doug asked.

"I was given only so much money to hire these people, and now they want to go on strike.

"What? In the middle of all this death and destruction these men want to go on strike?"

"They want more money."

"But we have no more money," Doug informed him. "We've spent everything. If they don't work, thousands will die. Well, can I talk to them?"

"It won't do any good. They're angry. Who knows what they'll do?"

Finally Doug's friend agreed. Walking over to an old burned-out school building, Doug climbed the steps, wondering what on earth he could say. Three hundred angry men surrounded the Rwandan who would act as interpreter. "Mr. Nichols wants to say something," he called above the clamor as Doug desperately searched for words that would get through to them.

"I can't possibly understand the pain you've experienced," Doug began, "and now, seeing your wives and children dying from cholera, I can never understand how that feels. Maybe you want more money for food and water and medical supplies for your families. I've never been in that position either. Nothing tragic has ever happened in my life that compares to what you've suffered. The only thing that's ever happened to me is that I've got cancer."

He was about to go on when the interpreter stopped. "Excuse me," he said, "did you say cancer?"

"Yes."

"And you came over here? Did your doctor say you could come?"

"He told me that if I came to Africa I'd probably be dead in three days."

"Your doctor told you that and you still came? What did you come for? And what if you die?"

"I'm here because God led us to come and do something for these people in his name," Doug told him. "I'm no hero. If I die, just bury me out in that field where you bury everybody else."

To Doug's utter amazement the man began to weep. Then, with tears flowing down his face, he turned back to the workers and began to preach. "This man has cancer," he told the crowd, which suddenly grew very quiet. In Rwanda, cancer is an automatic death sentence. "He came over here willing to die for our people," the interpreter continued, "and we're going on strike just to get a little bit more money? We should be ashamed!"

Suddenly men on all sides began falling to their knees in tears. Doug had no idea what was going on because no one had bothered to translate. To his great embarrassment, one fellow crawled over and threw his arms around Doug's legs. Dumbfounded, Doug watched as people stood to their feet, walked over to their stretchers, and went quietly back to work.

Later, as the interpreter recounted the whole story, Doug thought to himself, What did I do? Nothing. It wasn't my ability to care for the sick. It wasn't my ability to organize. All I did was get cancer. But God used that very weakness to move the hearts of people. Because they went back to work, thousands of lives were saved, and many heard the good news of Jesus Christ.[1]

APPENDIX 2

D r. Walter Kaiser, president of Gordon-Conwell Theological Seminary, writes: "In my judgment, the most dramatic moment in the entire 20th century came in 1946 when W. K. Wimsatt and Monroe Beardsley published their article 'The Intentional Fallacy' in The Sewanee Review" (Preaching and Teaching from the Old Testament, Baker 2003). Wimsatt and Beardsley, according to Kaiser's summary, taught that "whatever an author may have meant or intended to say by his or her written words is now irrelevant to the meanings we have come to assign as the meaning we see in the author's text. On this basis, the reader is the one who sets the meaning for the text." Also called "formalist criticism," this school argued, in short, that paying attention to the author's intentions is a fallacy.

I first encountered the idea 30 years ago—not in a philosophy class but in a graduate class on literary interpretation. This idea came through a professor who had been "infected" by her doctoral committee chairperson, who in turn had been influenced by literary critic Kenneth Burke. Twenty-five years after it was first presented, formalist criticism's hostility toward an author's intention had spread to many of the colleges that would educate the baby-boomer generation. Now, a half-century since it first was proclaimed, the Wimsatt-Beardsley doctrine, along with its children, is so widely accepted that it has tainted nearly all major social institutions—even the church.

One philosophical stalemate surfaced in the Senate over judicial nominations. Those who may never have heard of the "intentional fallacy" or the names of Wimsatt and Beardsley have nonetheless been indoctrinated in what has been called judicial activism. Judicial activism regards the Constitution of the United States as a "living document" that needs to be reinterpreted in each generation according to the zeitgeist—the milieu of needs, wishes, and politics of the day. Judicial activism was and is the vehicle for finding in the Constitution the rights of privacy and a woman's near-absolute right to abortion. It seeks continually to redefine the very words of our founding fathers, words that were chosen with the same care and precision with which they were written with quills by hand on parchment. We cannot, judicial activists argue, really know what the founding fathers meant, and even when we do know, that intent is secondary to our current situation.

As a result, otherwise qualified nominees for federal courts have been quashed on the grounds that they are "outside the judicial mainstream"—a cryptic phrase for describing, for example, people who do not believe that the Constitution provides the absolute right of abortion. The message is clear: If you don't believe that the Constitution protects a woman's absolute right to make reproductive choices, you are "out of the mainstream" because you oppose the "law of the land" (as expressed not by legislation but by case law determined by five of nine justices at a particular point in time).

Standing guard on this hill are the "strict constructionists." Viewed as dinosaurs by activists, they regard the Constitution as a sacred trust, continually asking the question dismissed by Wimsatt and Beardsley: What did the authors of the Constitution intend? They seek to interpret the document with a commitment to the truest meaning of integrity.

A few miles northwest of Capitol Hill, the Washington National Cathedral is set on another hill overlooking the city. It is a symbolic center of the Episcopal Church U.S.A. Here, a slightly different strain of the intentional fallacy has been manifested among a group of people who historically were established on the words of the Bible (and the Book of Common Prayer).

The result is that Anglicans all over the world are at war over the elevation of an openly noncelibate gay man to bishop of New Hampshire. Supporters of the new bishop downplay the matter, insisting that the rest of the church will get used to a gay bishop over time, just as it eventually became accustomed to female priests. But the issue is clearly different. This is not a debate over a high-profile, but otherwise secondary, theological point (secondary in that it does not deal with issues of the nature of God, the person of Christ, or salvation). Like the strict constitutional constructionists, Episcopal conservatives divide from the supporters of the gay bishop at deep fault lines.

These Episcopal conservatives read the Bible and seek to interpret it by determining, as best they are able, the intended meaning of the text. They will not always agree about the intended meaning of particular passages, but they desire to know and be faithful to the original meaning of the biblical text.

But in the Episcopal Church, the effect of "The Intentional Fallacy" can clearly be seen. Those who have embraced this fallacious philosophy of interpretation apply their flawed hermeneutic to important biblical passages that speak of God's judgments over homosexuality (Gen. 19, Lev. 18, Rom. 1:24-32), and come away saying that homosexuality is good and even blessed by God. To do this, these church leaders must buy into the idea that it doesn't matter what the Bible writers meant. Gene Robinson, the newly ordained gay bishop, put it this way: "Just simply to say that it goes against tradition and the teaching of the church and Scripture does not necessarily make it wrong."

This same disregard for the authorial intent of the church's authoritative words has been witnessed elsewhere. In March, a United Methodist court acquitted openly gay pastor Karen Dammann of charges that she was in violation of the denomination's laws regarding homosexual practice. The jury said the Methodist Book of Discipline was unclear in stating, "Homosexual practice is incompatible with church teaching." The jury doubted whether those words were intended to be a formal declaration of the church and whether they should be regarded as church law.

Among Presbyterians (PCUSA) it goes like this: Stephen Van Kuiken, former pastor of Mount Auburn Presbyterian Church in Cincinnati, was convicted in 2003 of performing a same-sex marriage. A church court had warned him not to do so. The Presbytery of Cincinnati rebuked and removed Van Kuiken, who lost his ordination and membership in the PCUSA. When, in February of this year, a synod court restored his ordination, it cited a 2000 decision by the denomination's Permanent Judicial Commission: "While [saying] that same-sex marriages are impermissible," the ruling states, the 2000 decision "avoids an outright prohibition by using the words 'should' and 'should not.'" What part of impermissible do they not understand?

Here we see steps taken beyond formalist criticism, an offspring of the intentional fallacy. Not only is an author's intention bypassed, but the clear meaning of the naked words is also ignored. Evangelicals of all denominations who stand firmly committed to the Word of God—and to the plain meaning of words in their churches' fundamental documents—are rightly alarmed at such cavalier disregard for truth. The hostility to authorial intention, born in academe, is a deadly virus that seems to be spreading.

Evangelicals are seeing the alarming results of this disease in two of the three institutions God ordained—the church and the government. The third institution, the family, is also being dismantled by both those in the church and those in the government who have embraced "The Intentional Fallacy" and extended it into postmodernism. The attempts to redefine marriage as something other than the union of a man and a woman for a lifetime are consistent with the implication that, in the end, words have no intrinsic meaning.

A skeptic once asked me: "If God is all powerful, can he make a square circle?" The question points to a categorical impossibility. Yet there are in our world those who would, for the sake of their agenda, seek to give us "gay marriage." Marriage by definition, however, has always involved a man and a woman. Stripped of conventional meaning or even the possibility of conventional denotations, words can take on the value of junk bonds.

In its front-page story on the decision of the Massachusetts Supreme Judicial Court, which struck down the ban on same-sex marriage, The Washington Post noted: "Chief Justice Margaret H. Marshall wrote the 4 to 3 majority opinion, which acknowledged that it was finding in the words of John Adams a meaning that he could hardly have foreseen when he wrote the Massachusetts Constitution 223 years ago." One must wonder if those who embrace and apply the intentional fallacy and its children grasp the implications of reducing language—including their own—to a level of meaninglessness.

The professor who introduced me to this odious doctrine gave us a midterm examination. In order to express my disdain for the concept, I simply wrote an answer to a totally different question than she had asked. I got a zero on the question, of course, and used a follow-up visit to her office to challenge her doctrine of intentional fallacy. She told me I had not answered the question she wrote. I responded that once she had written the question, I had no need to determine what she—the author—originally intended. I had interpreted the question as I had wanted. Trying to determine what she intended by the question, I argued, was a fallacy.

My professor was clearly angry because she was not yet, in 1973, a fully postmodern woman. A fully postmodern woman would have found a consistent worldview unnecessary. Today's postmoderns—from judicial activists to the friends of the gay Episcopal bishop—find in the writings of Professor Richard Rorty of Stanford University the essence of the paradoxical postmodern perspective. Rorty argues that what is needed is "a repudiation of the very idea of anything . . . having an intrinsic nature to be expressed or represented"—except, of course, his own ideas. There can be no distinction between a true meaning of words and a false one, because "truth is not out there"—except his truth.

To be sure, Wimsatt and Beardsley's article may or may not be the most dramatic moment of the 20th century. But it was certainly one of a number of events that declared war on the idea that the articulation of truth depends on words having specific meaning and on knowing with some certainty what an author intended. This is not only a religious issue—the very fabric of our culture is at stake. In both government and church, the stakes could not be higher. These are two hills worth dying on.[1]

ABOUT THE AUTHOR

Since 2006 Bob Wenz has been seeking—with some limitations—to serve the kingdom of God in a variety of ways under the umbrella of Renewing Total Worship Ministries (www.rtwministries. com); as a part-time professor of philosophy at a community college; as a part-time seminary professor; as an author; as a preaching coach; and as a board member of the National Association of Evangelicals..

This follows twenty-five years of pastoral ministry (in Lansing, MI; Covina, CA; Clifton Park, NY; and Washington, DC) and three years of service with the National Association of Evangelicals as vice-president of national ministries, which prompted a relocation to the rarefied air of Colorado Springs (6,834 feet) in 2005.

A graduate of Arizona State University, with both bachelor's and master's degrees in speech communication, Bob went on for theological studies at Trinity Evangelical Divinity School and completed his doctor of ministry degree at Bethel University of St. Paul, Minnesota, where his dissertation focused on training lay people to share their faith in Christ.

Bob is the author of *Room for God? A Worship Challenge for the Church Growth and Marketing Era* (Baker Books 1994, reprinted in 2007 by Total Worship Ministries) and is also a regular contributor to *Christianity Today* and other publications.

Bob was ordained by the Conservative Congregational Christian

Conference and is also credentialed with the Christian and Missionary Alliance.

Since 1987 he has taught and preached in more than forty countries throughout Europe, Asia, Africa, South America, and the Pacific Islands—including Indonesia. Bob and his wife, Suellen, a senior editor for Compassion International, are in their fourth decade of their journey together. They have a college-aged son and a married daughter—and a spectacular granddaughter.

NOTES

Chapter 1: Our Need for Anchors

1. "The Solid Rock," music and lyrics by Ruth C. Jones, 1944.
2. Anne Rice, *Christ the Lord: Out of Egypt* (New York: Knopf, 2005), presents a fictional and somewhat insightful account of what Jesus would have been thinking as a child growing up. I don't necessarily recommend the work, but it does raise significantly our awareness and curiosity about what Jesus might have been like and might have been thinking as God in immature human flesh.
3. We ought not to assume that Jesus simply had a divine download of data, but rather that he learned the Word of God by study, as other children. According to some historians, a rabbi would have memorized the Torah or perhaps even the entire Tenach (Old Testament).
4. M. Scott Peck, *The Road Less Traveled* (New York: Touchstone, 1978), 15–17.

Chapter 2: Preparing for the Kairos Moment

1. "It was the best of times, it was the worst of times," is, of course, from Dickens's *Tale of Two Cities.* "It was a dark and stormy night" is a cliché of literature made most famous by Charles Schultz and his character Snoopy. In fact, the Edward Bulwer-Lytton Award for the best deliberately bad opening line is granted annually in honor of the author who wrote that cliché in 1830.
2. See Harold W. Hoehner, *Chronological Aspects of the Life of Christ* (Grand Rapids, MI: Zondervan, 1977), 95.
3. Ibid., 65.
4. John 11:48: "If we let him go on like this, everyone will believe in him, and then the Romans will come and take away both our place and our nation."
5. Around the time of the premiere of the *Passion of the Christ*, I took part on National Public Radio in a nationally broadcast radio program debate concerning the film and its alleged anti-Semitism. The debate was joined by a well-known columnist for the *Boston Globe* (a former Roman Catholic priest who was disgruntled

with his former church and with Mel Gibson for his devotion to the traditional Catholic teachings and traditions). The former priest argued that Christianity, or at least Catholicism, had become a "bloody religion" that had instigated both anti-Semitism and violence (especially the Crusades and the Inquisition) since the time it came under the influence of Anselm nearly one thousand years ago. Christianity never had much to do with the cross historically, he asserted; that was a "modern aberration," and the continual focus in the post-Anselm church on the cross was the cause of Christianity's misguided violence and historic anti-Semitism (hostility toward the Christ killers). My reply was simple: "Paul the apostle, who predates Anselm by one thousand years, said, 'For I resolved to *know nothing* while I was with you except Jesus Christ and him crucified.'" The former priest is woefully mistaken. Our faith rests on a *repulsive reality*—Jesus Christ, and him crucified.

6. From personal conversation. As a twenty-year-old with a life expectancy of seventy years, each day represented 1/18,000 of my remaining life. As I write this at age sixty, each day represents 1/3,650 of my remaining life if I live to my seventieth birthday.

7. Daniel P. Mannix, *The History of Torture* (New York: Dell, 1964).

8. Fouad Ajami, "The Son of Ayatollah," *U.S. News and World Report* (May 22, 2006): 36.

9. Jay Tolson, "Special Report: Aiming for Apocalypse," *U.S. News and World Report* (May 22, 2006): 35.

10. According to the dispensational view of the last days (*eschatology*) there will be seven years of upheaval on the earth prior to the end of history and God's final judgment. This "seventieth week of Jacob's trouble"—called the great tribulation—begins with the removal of the church from the world in the rapture, followed by two intervals of three and a half years. The first is a time of tribulation; the second is marked by an outpouring of God wrath. The first season is characterized by *thlipsis*, or tribulation (the very thing that Jesus said his followers would have in this world). The second season of these final days of human history is described as *orge*, or wrath. These seasons correspond to the two halves of the "great tribulation." Paul told the believers in Thessalonica that they were waiting for God's Son, Jesus, "from heaven, whom he raised from the dead—Jesus, *who rescues us from the coming wrath*" (1 Thess. 1:10; *orge* not *thlipsis*). And he added, "For God did not appoint us to suffer *wrath* but to receive salvation through our Lord Jesus Christ" (1 Thess.5:9). We would be exempt from the *wrath* of God to come but never exempted from *tribulation*—whether the generic but very real tribulation that abounds today or the great tribulation that is yet to come.

Notes

Chapter 3: Anchor 1: Learning Who We Are (Part 1)

1. Townshend almost sounds as though he were addressing Jesus when he writes of love falling from the trees, when he acknowledges that he spews forth sewage, and that he feels best on his knees. He expresses his awe that he would "still receive your kiss" and that there is "such a love as this."

2. Eric H. Ericson, *Identity and the Life Cycle* (New York: W. W. Norton, 1980).

3. Lisa McLeod, "Cracking 'The Code' on Love, Fear," *The Gwinnett Daily Post*, May 26, 2006, Viewpoints.

4. The Nicene Creed, http://www.creeds.net/ancient/nicene.htm.

5. *Ancient History Sourcebook: Pliny and Trajan: Correspondence, c. 112 CE,* http://www.fordham.edu/halsall/ancient/pliny-trajan1.html (accessed August 10, 2009).

6. http://www.religion-online.org/showarticle.asp?title=385 (accessed August 12, 2009).

7. Thomas Merton, *Seeds of Contemplation*, (New York: New Direction Books, 1961), 32–35.

8. Dallas Willard, *The Divine Conspiracy: Rediscovering Our Hidden Life in God* (New York: HarperCollins, 1998). In chapter 2, Willard introduces and fully develops the concept of sin management. This idea has been picked up by numerous authors and has entered into the Christian lexicon.

9. I believe these concepts came from Dr. Vernon Grounds, now chancellor of Denver Seminary.

10. Paul Tournier, *To Understand Each Other: Classic Wisdom on Marriage,* translated by John S. Gilmour (Louisville, KY: John Knox Press, 1967).

11. Mark Regnerus, "The Case for Early Marriage," http://www.christianitytoday.com/ct/2009/august/16.22.html.

12. Peck, *The Road Less Traveled*, 19–24.

Chapter 4: Anchor 1: Learning Who We Are (Part 2)

1. William Glasser, *Reality Therapy: A New Approach to Psychiatry* (San Francisco, CA: Harper and Row, 1965), 9.

2. Glasser, *Reality Therapy*, 8.

3. The catechism states: "The chief end of man is to glorify God and enjoy him forever." Piper adapted it, and I think did so appropriately. See "Passion for the Supremacy of God. Part 1" at Desiring God Ministries, http://www.desiringgod.org/ResourceLibrary/ConferenceMessages/ByDate/1997/1906_Passion_for_the_Supremacy_of_God_Part_1/.

4. Henri Nouwen, *In the Name of Jesus*, cited in Glen Packiam, *Secondhand Jesus: Trading Rumors of God for a Firsthand Faith* (Colorado Springs, CO: David C.

Cook, 2009), 22–23.

5. http://www.skyandtelescope.com/news/3306251.html (accessed July 12, 2010).

Chapter 5: Anchor 2: Learning Who Is in Control of Our Lives
1. Royce G. Gruenler, *The Trinity in the Gospel of John: A Thematic Commentary on the Fourth Gospel,* unpublished manuscript (1986).
2. Dietrich Bonhoeffer, *Creation and Fall: Temptation* (New York: MacMillan, 1983), 122–23.
3. http://www.tenth.org/articles/000507jmb.pdf (accessed August 14, 2008).

Chapter 6: Anchor 3: Grasping the Truth of God's Word
1. Psalm 19:1–4.
2. William Stuntz, "Three Gifts for Hard Times," *Christianity Today,* August 2009, http://www.christianitytoday.com/ct/2009/august/34.44.html (accessed August 19, 2009).
3. The 1970s was marked by a renewed debate among evangelicals about the nature of the Bible, highlighted by Harold Lindsell's *The Battle for the Bible* (Grand Rapids: Zondervan, 1976).
4. My unpublished master's thesis "Expository Preaching as a Unique form of Pulpit Address," (Arizona State University, 1974) sought to distinguish expository or expositional preaching from the earlier form of textual preaching that sought to dissect significant verses and sometimes ordinary ones. Like the allegorical approach, textual and/or topical preaching depend on the invention (spiritual illumination) of the preacher.
5. *Flashpoints,* PBS. See my Web site: www.rtwministries.com.
6. Agape Press, http://headlines.agapepress.org/archive/11/32003a.asp (accessed August 4, 2008, page no longer available).
7. See Appendix 2.
8. Brian Lowery, "Biblical Literacy Reaches New Low," http://www.outofur.com/archives/2009/01/biblical_litera.html.
9. See Gary M. Burge, "The Greatest Story Never Read: Recovering Biblical Literacy in the Church," August 9, 1999, ChristianityTodayLibrary.com http://www.ctlibrary.com/ct/1999/august9/9t9045.html (accessed February 14, 2008) and Michael J. Vlach, "Crisis in America's Churches: Bible Knowledge at All-Time Low," TheologicalStudies.com, http://www.theologicalstudies.org/page/page/1573625.htm (accessed August 9, 2008).
10. The Barna Group, "Religious Beliefs Vary Widely By Denomination," June 2001, http://www.barna.org/barna-update/article/5-barna-update/53-religious-

beliefs-vary-widely-by-denomination (accessed July 29, 2010).

11. David F. Wells, *No Place for Truth or Whatever Happened to Evangelical Theology?* (Grand Rapids, MI: Eerdmans, 1993), 4.

12. The Barna Group, "New Book Describes the State of the Church in 2002," June 2002, http://www.barna.org/barna-update/article/5-barna-update/75-new-book-describes-the-state-of-the-church-in-2002 (accessed July 29, 2010).

13. http://www.yesselman.com/SpinIdea.htm#evolves#evolves (accessed August 12, 2008).

14. The theory begins with the idea that Genesis 1 and Genesis 2 present two different versions of the creation, evidence that the Scriptures were compiled at a later date from two different oral traditions. The alleged dual accounts of the flood in Genesis 6 have been used as the primer to teach JEPD. The Graff-Wellhausen hypothesis is as widely held as doctrine (not hypothesis, in spite of the lack of external evidence) by the Catholic Church as well as the neo-orthodox theologians and some who would call themselves evangelicals.

Wellhausen, in particular, conceived of Israel's religion not as a revealed faith from God beginning with Abraham, Isaac, and Jacob (Israel), but beginning with animism and evolving through polytheism to henotheism and finally to monotheism at the time of later prophets. This idea—that the Bible thus is a product of human, evolutionary development—emerges not surprisingly from the age of Darwin when it was in vogue to apply evolutionary processes to almost anything. The Bible is to be seen as a history of the evolution of a tribal religion without any revelation, a view diametrically opposite to the Bible's own declarations concerning itself (2 Tim 3:16). While modern scholarship has modified Graff-Wellhausen, the general impact of this theory upon biblical theology remains.

According to the documentary hypothesis developed by Graff and Wellhausen, the J document appeared about 1000 BC, produced by a writer whose interest was in Hebron. This was revised by J about 950 in the interest of making an appeal to the people of the north after their rebellion against the house of David. The E document is much the same as J. It was written about 700 and represents an attempted rapprochement between the north and the south. After the fall of Jerusalem in 586, another rapprochement was attempted through the conflating of J and E in which effort was made to preserve the salient features of each. The Deuteronomic Code was designed to provide authoritative guidance for the people of the north after the catastrophe of 722. It was accepted by the south after 586 and later combined with JE. The Priestly Code was drawn up by those who wished to make Jerusalem the religious center of Israel after the return from captivity.

From Chester Lehman, *Biblical Theology: Old Testament* (Scottdale, PA: Herald Press, 1971), chapter 1. Used by permission.

15. Ben Witherington III, *The Jesus Quest: The Third Search for the Jew of Nazareth* (Downers Grove: InterVarsity, 1995), 9.

16. From the author's class notes from Carl F. H. Henry: ST721 Contemporary Theology (Trinity Evangelical Divinity School, October 1974).

17. http://virtualreligion.net/forum/ (accessed August 11, 2008).

18. Postmodernism repudiates the corresponding theory of truth because postmoderns mistakenly associate it with the Enlightenment and modernism. They offer instead an epistemological relativism that renders all ideas equal and denies an objective truth. When all truths are "equal," propositional truth has been supplanted by what amounts to mere opinion. We are at risk of proclaiming a faith devoid of truth or simply in search of truth—and either we don't realize it or don't care. McLaren said himself that "I understand why people often accuse me . . . of pluralistic relativism" and that to refer to him as a relativist is to misunderstand or misrepresent his position.

19. Jeremy Green, Denver Seminary online journal, September 1, 2005, http://www.denverseminary.edu/article/a-generous-orthodoxy-review-by-jeremy-green/ (accessed August 2008).

20. Ibid.

21. Gary Gilley, "Everything Must Change by Brian McLaren," Southern Valley Chapel, http://www.svchapel.org/resources/book-reviews/4-christian-living/635-everything-must-change-by-brian-mclaren (accessed July 13, 2010).

22. Brian McLaren, *A New Kind of Christianity: Ten Questions That Are Transforming the Faith* (New York: HarperCollins, 2010).

23. http://www.icelebz.com/quotes/saint_augustine/

24. Foucault wrote, "My position is that . . . as soon as one 'proposes'—one proposes a vocabulary, an ideology, which can only have effects of domination. ["Confinement, psychiatry, prison" in L. Kritzman, (ed.), *Politics, Philosophy, Culture: Interviews and Other Writings, 1977-1984.* (New York: Routledge), 197].

He added: "Who are we, we who speak a language such that it has powers that are imposed on us in our society as well as on other societies? What is this language which can be turned against us which we can turn against ourselves? What is this incredible obsession with the passage to the universal in Western discourse?" [http://www.michel-foucault.com/quote/2005q.html].

25. Fredrick Nietzsche, *Twilight of the Idols* (1895), trans. Walter Kaufmann and R. J. Hollingdale, http://www.handprint.com/SC/NIE/GotDamer.html.

Notes

26. "When *I* use a word," Humpty Dumpty said in rather a scornful tone, "it means just what I choose it to mean—neither more nor less."

"The question is," said Alice, "whether you *can* make words mean so many different things."

"The question is," said Humpty Dumpty, "which is to be master—that's all."

From Chapter VI of *Through the Looking Glass* by Lewis Carroll (Lothrop Publishing, 1898), 164.

27. John Eldredge, *Wild at Heart: Discovering the Secret of a Man's Soul* (Nashville: Thomas Nelson, 2001), 3–4.

28. David Rea and Carlton Wynne *Wild at Heart: A Critique*, http://www.ouruf. org/d/cvt_wildatheart.pdf (accessed April 30, 2010).

Chapter 7: Anchor 4: Learning to Pray Again

1. John Piper, *Prayer: The Work of Missions*, ACMC Annual Meeting, Denver, CO, July 29, 1988, http://www.desiringgod.org/ResourceLibrary/ConferenceMessages/ByDate/1988/1459_Prayer_The_Work_of_Missions/ (accessed April 30, 2010).

2. C. S. Lewis, *Letters to Malcolm: Chiefly on Prayer* (New York: Harcourt, 1963), 114.

3. Ibid., 113–115.

4. David Wells, "Rebelling Against the Status Quo," quoted in *Perspectives on the World Christian Movement,* eds. Ralph Winter and Steve Hawthorne (Pasadena, CA: William Carey Library, 1982), 142–45.

5. Margaret Manning, "The Problem of Unanswered Prayer," *A Slice of Infinity,* September 2, 2008, Ravi Zacharias International Ministries, http://www.rzim. org/resources/read/asliceofinfinity/todaysslice.aspx?aid=10085 (accessed May 3, 2010.) Quote of M. Craig Barnes from *When God Interrupts* (Downers Grove: InterVarsity, 1996), 124–125.

6. Ibid.

Chapter 8: Anchor 5: Following Our Guide

1. From personal e-mail, January 2005. Ed Landry is a cancer surviver who continues with his wife, Janet, to serve God in the Philippines with Action International Ministries as they have since 1984.

2. This story was told by Leakey in a television interview which I saw several years ago, and which was several years after his death in 1972. Of course when I heard the story I didn't think I would ever wish I had recorded the name and the date of the program for a footnote thirty years later. But I attest to the accuracy of the story because I retold the story not long after and have my detailed sermon notes

from circa 1985.

3. J. Carter Johnson, "Deliver Us from Kony," *Christianity Today* (January 2006), http://www.christianitytoday.com/ct/2006/january/18.30.html (accessed May 3, 2010).

4. From transcript: *Opening the Door to Luther* [Video of the Lutheran Church in America], http://www.ricksteves.com/about/pressroom/activism/luther.htm (accessed July 29, 2010).

5. Erik Reece, "Jesus Without the Miracles—Thomas Jefferson's Bible and the Gospel of Thomas," *Harper's Magazine*, December 1, 2005. http://www.mindfully.org/Reform/2005/Jesus-Without-Miracles1dec05.htm (accessed August 2009).

6. Eric Metaxas' excellent biography *Bonhoeffer: Pastor, Martyr, Prophet, Spy* [Nashville: Thomas Nelson, 2010] clearly chronicles this sad page in church history.

7. *Evangelicals and Catholics Together: Toward a Common Mission*, eds. Charles Colson and Richard J. Neuhaus (Nashville: Thomas Nelson, 1995) has now been in circulation for fifteen years. After a wave of initial discussion, there seems to have been little movement toward a unified theology.

8. Betsy Childs, "The King's Perspective," *A Slice of Infinity*, January 17, 2006, http://www.rzim.org/resources/read/asliceofinfinity/todaysslice.aspx?aid=8977 (accessed May 4, 2010).

9. I had the opportunity to teach systematic theology to a group of Russian students in Moscow a few years ago. They were delightful, hungry to learn, and very much needing to learn. They had good knowledge of biblical content but very little theological understanding. The first day of class, I was startled by the question of a student: "Excuse me, Professor, but what do you think of the heresy of Calvinism?"

It took me half of the afternoon to discover the source of the bias of the Russian students against what they perceived as the antinomianism (the idea that because I am under grace I have no obligation at all to the law of God) of Calvinism. This has been a problematic misunderstanding for more than a hundred years, the result of some hyper-Calvinist groups that took root in Mother Russia. It then took me the other half of the afternoon to help them see the merits and value of Calvinism—and that Calvinists love Jesus too. (They agreed later with my thesis that the results of sin in our lives are pervasive. I told them that by believing in the doctrine of total depravity, they were now good "one-point" Calvinists.) They needed guidance into all truth that the Holy Spirit brings, and as they embraced the Word of God, they began to move out of their comfort zones and past their biases into "new truths" that were there all the time.

10. Gordon D. Fee and Douglas Stuart have made a great contribution to our pursuit of the right understanding of God's Word with *How to Read the Bible for All Its Worth*, 3rd ed.(1981, 1993, Grand Rapids, MI: Zondervan, 2003).

11. Walter C. Kaiser Jr., *Toward an Exegetical Theology: Biblical Exegesis for Preaching and Teaching* (Grand Rapids, MI: Baker, 1981), 20.

12. Quoted by Dr. Graham Cole, Principal of Ridley College Melbourne, in "Preaching Christ in a Post-modern World," Perspective 2000 Vol. 8 No. 1 [http://perspective.org.au/preaching/69/preaching-christ-in-a-postmodern-world].

13. Sadly, archives of the *Wittenburg Door* in the 1970s are incomplete, and no index of articles is available to search for the original publication from which this statement was taken.

14. I believe that we will be on a new, recreated earth, where we will be restored to the purpose God originally had for Adam—to walk with him and be co-creators and caretakers of his creation. (For more on this, I recommend Michael Eugene Wittmer's insightful *Heaven Is a Place on Earth: Why Everything You Do Matters to God*.)

15. Viktor E. Frankl, *Man's Search for Meaning* (1959, Boston: Beacon Press, 2006), 74. Frankl added: "Usually this happened quite suddenly, in the form of a crisis, the symptoms of which were familiar to the experienced camp inmate. We all feared this moment—not for ourselves, which would have been pointless, but for our friends. Usually it began with the prisoner refusing one morning to get dressed and wash or to go out on the parade grounds. No entreaties, no blows, no threats had any effect. He just lay there, hardly moving. If this crisis was brought about by an illness, he refused to be taken to the sick-bay or to do anything to help himself. He simply gave up. There he remained, lying in his own excreta, and nothing bothered him any more."

16. Interstitial pulmonary fibrosis—stage four of sarcoidosis—is a disease whereby scar tissue forms in the interstitial areas of the lungs, preventing the exchange of oxygen and carbon dioxide.

17. Quoted in Gary Keisling, *Relentless Spirituality: Embracing the Spiritual Disciplines of A. B. Simpson* (Camp Hill, PA: WingSpread Publishers, 2004), 8–11. Citing A. B. Simpson, unpublished poem, "Breathing Out and Breathing In" (Colorado Springs, CO: A. B. Simpson Historical Library, n.d.). Used by permission.

Chapter 9: Admonition 1: Trust (The Antidote for a Troubled Heart)
1. John Piper, from e-mail forwarded by the church to friends of Bethlehem

Baptist, January 9, 2006.

2. Paul Tillich, *The Courage to Be*, 2nd. ed. (1952, New Haven, CT: Yale University Press, 2000), 40–42.

3. Frank Lake, *Clinical Theology: A Theological and Psychological Basis to Clinical Pastoral Care*, abridged by Martin Yeomans (New York: Crossroads Publishing, 1987), 13.

4. Kenneth Kantzer, "John Calvin and the Mystery of the Trinity," in *Trinity Voices* (Deerfield, IL: Trinity Evangelical Divinity School, n.d.).

5. John Koster, *The Atheist Syndrome* (Brentwood, TN: Wolgemuth and Hyatt, 1989).

6. Lake, *Clinical Theology*.

7. Jeff VanVonderen, *Tired of Trying to Measure Up: Getting Free from the Demands, Expectations, and Intimidation of Well-Meaning People* (Minneapolis, MN: Bethany House, 1985).

8. In Job 42:7 God told Eliphaz that he and his friend were wrong when they spoke on this subject.

9. Read more of Bill's story in "What It Costs to Reach the Community: An interview with Bill Leslie," by Marshall Shelley and Larry Weeden, *Leadership Journal* (Summer 1988), http://www.christianitytoday.com/le/1988/summer/8813012. html (accessed May 7, 2010).

Chapter 10: Admonition 2: Watch Out (The Dangers of Pride and Foolishness)

1. A.C. Green confirmed my memory of his appearance on the Phil Donohue Show though personal correspondence, 2010.

2. Marvin Rosenthal, *The Pre-Wrath Rapture of the Church* (Nashville, TN: Thomas Nelson, 1990).

Chapter 11: Linking Our Anchors and Jesus' Admonitions

1. C. S. Lewis, *A Grief Observed* (San Francisco, CA: HarperCollins, 1966), 3, 37, 38.

2. Darlene Deibler Rose, *Evidence Not Seen: A Woman's Miraculous Faith in the Jungles of World War II* (San Francisco: Harper & Row, 1988), 155–156.

Appendix 1

1. Phil Callaway, *Who Put My Life on Fast-Forward? How to Slow Down and Start Living Again* (Eugene, OR: Harvest House, 2002), 228-234. Used by permission.

Appendix 2

1. *Christianity Today* 48, no. 7 (July 2004): 46. Used by permission.